Diane D. Knott

STRIP
QUILT
SECRETS

5 Techniques • 15 Projects

C&T PUBLISHING

Text copyright © 2018 by Diane D. Knott

Photography and artwork copyright © 2018 by C&T Publishing, Inc.

Publisher: Amy Marson

Creative Director: Gailen Runge

Acquisitions Editor: Roxane Cerda

Managing Editor: Liz Aneloski

Editor: Christine Doyle

Technical Editor: Helen Frost

Cover/Book Designer: April Mostek

Production Coordinator: Tim Manibusan

Production Editor: Alice Mace Nakanishi

Illustrator: Freesia Pearson Blizard

Photo Assistants: Rachel Holmes and Mai Yong Vang

Photography by Mai Yong Vang and Kelly Burgoyne
of C&T Publishing, Inc., unless otherwise noted

Published by C&T Publishing, Inc., P.O. Box 1456, Lafayette, CA 94549

Library of Congress Cataloging-in-Publication Data

Names: Knott, Diane D., 1966- author.

Title: Strip quilt secrets : 5 techniques, 15 projects / Diane D. Knott.

Description: Lafayette, CA : C&T Publishing, Inc., [2018] | Includes index.

Identifiers: LCCN 2018009854 | ISBN 9781617457579 (soft cover)

Subjects: LCSH: Patchwork--Patterns. | Quilting--Patterns.

Classification: LCC TT835 .K5855 2018 | DDC 746.46/041--dc23

LC record available at https://lccn.loc.gov/2018009854

Printed in China

10 9 8 7 6 5 4 3 2

DEDICATION

In loving memory of Patsy Eckman, who told me I needed to write a book showing her what to do with all those strips she had collected.

To my family and special friends. Thank you for the love and support and never-ending laughter.

SPECIAL THANKS

The Warm Company generously provided all the batting for these quilts.

Cheryl Ashley-Serafine and Millie Rondon, thank you so much for your gorgeous machine quilting and your friendship.

Christine Doyle, Liz Aneloski, and Helen Frost, thank you for your hard work and attention to detail.

CONTENTS

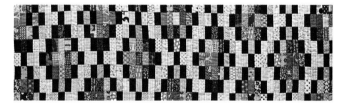

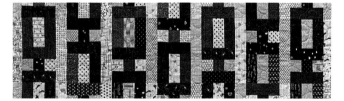

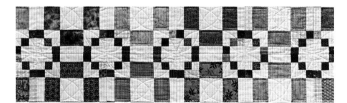

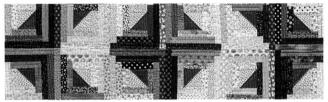

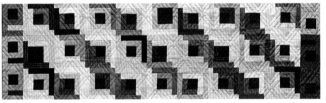
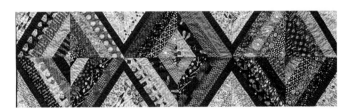

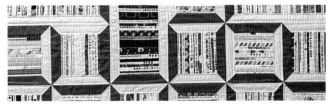

"What do I do with all these fabric strips?" It's a common question I hear when teaching and visiting with quilters. Let's face it, we all collect fabric strips whether we want to or not. We have leftover pieces from finished projects, lengths of extra binding, remains from precuts, and the last bits of yardage that go unused. So what are we to do with them? Plenty of patterns and books on the market have super-simple strip-piecing quilts. This book takes a different approach. Quilts can be made from strips without looking like they were just stitched together in a hurry. I've got a few secrets I would like to share with you that will help turn your strips into fun and interesting quilts.

If I'm being completely honest, the term *strip quilt* makes me cringe a little. We live in an era of "quick and easy" and "make it fast" and "get it done now." While those ideas and concepts may be helpful, even motivational or inspiring to some folks, that's really not how I want to make my quilts. Of course, I want to use the best techniques for accuracy and ease while I'm quilting. I also want to use all the tools available to achieve the best results, and I certainly don't want to make the process harder than it needs to be! However, I want to make quilts that sparkle, provide interest, and share the beauty of great design. I want to make quilts that are as comforting to look at as they are to use.

That being said, I am a scrap quilter at heart. I love the idea of creating something wonderful out of the bits and pieces available. I don't want any fabric to go unused or unappreciated. The challenge then becomes how do I use all the fabric I have and still create quilts that are beautiful and meaningful?

With these quilts, I hope to share the methods for getting the most effective use from your fabric, simple techniques that result in accurate piecing, tips for making every step more efficient, and stunning quilts that will be treasured forever but don't take years to finish. I hope that this book inspires you to look at your fabric in a new way, consider some new ideas, and learn some new techniques. If these things happen, you are sure to enjoy this book as much as I have enjoyed writing it and creating the quilts.

Enjoy every stitch,

GETTING STARTED

With the advent of the rotary cutter and ruler system, cutting strips accurately and quickly became possible and making quilts from those strips was inevitable. You need to know some things before getting started, and if you read through these methods and tips, you'll find that what to avoid is just as important as what to remember. Whether you are starting with yardage cut from the bolt, fat quarters, scraps, or salvaged fabric from old shirts or other sources, modern methods and accurate techniques will make both the process enjoyable and the results fabulous.

THE FABRIC

Whether you collect fabric from yard sales, salvage fabric from old clothes, shop online, or visit your local quilt shop, let's discuss the fabric.

Old Fabrics

Using and reusing fabrics from clothing or other projects is a great way to recycle! However, keep a few tips in mind to make the process of incorporating these fabrics into your stash much easier.

Always wash items that you plan to use! Even if it's just been in storage for years, if the fabric is going to disintegrate during its first washing, you want to know that before you spend the time sewing it into your quilt. Not all dyes and fabrics are created equal—some will not withstand the test of time—and knowing that before

you put them into your quilt is vital. So wash and dry them as you plan to do with the finished quilt.

Once the fabrics (or clothes or other items) are washed and dried, press them. Some items have mystery ingredients that may not be labeled. If polyester or nylon threads are present, find out now by pressing. These fabrics will melt under the cotton setting on the iron. Again, it's better to find out now rather than later. Using other fiber content in a quilt is okay, it's just important to know ahead of time.

⭐ TIP Protect Your Iron

Use a thin muslin pressing cloth to protect the iron if you suspect questionable content in a fabric.

New Fabrics

As for new fabrics, I never wash them. Shopping at local quilt stores will ensure quality fabrics that should wash without bleeding of colors. Most importantly, using new, unwashed fabrics will create the crinkled look of a vintage quilt once it is freshly washed and warm from the dryer.

Also, using new fabrics that are unwashed makes them easier to handle, sew, cut, and press. The sizing included in the manufacturing helps keep them from fraying. Combining washed fabrics with new fabrics will work. Use a pressing spray for washed fabrics to give them the same body as the unwashed fabrics for easier handling.

 Catching Colors

If you do have a color that runs on a quilt, safety pin a color catching laundry sheet to the affected spot and rewash.

Buying Fabric

Most of the time I buy fat quarters. If I like the color or pattern and simply want it, a fat quarter will do! Fat quarter bundles are even better! If it looks like a good border or "feature" fabric (a great color combination or large print) I buy 2½ yards. I've never met a border that needed to be longer than that. If it's a bargain I can't pass up, I get 5 yards for a backing. I may not save it all for a backing, but at least I will have enough if I choose to use it that way. I also love pieced backings, so I never hesitate to add a strip of something to an otherwise plain backing.

Fabric Organization and Storage

Almost every time I teach I get asked the age-old question, "How do you organize your stash?" While I don't claim to have the best system in the world for storage and organization, I do have a system that works well for me. It's evolved over the years as my stash has evolved. Maybe it's time for you to consider how you store your stash and make some adjustments to see if you can create a system that works better for you. I find that having fabric stored in a way that keeps it ready to use works best for me.

Yardage

In my stash, yardage gets folded and placed in piles according to color on shelves. I tend to use this fabric on a regular basis, so I need it easily accessible. I found when I kept larger cuts in bins, I forgot what I had and the fabrics didn't get used. Seeing them helps me to better use what I have before buying more. When less than 1 yard remains, it goes into the drawer storage system I use for smaller cuts and fat quarters.

Fat Quarters

Pretty bundles remain on open shelving until they are broken into. Once I open the bundle and begin using it, the remainder is added to my fat quarter storage by color. I do not keep fabric lines together once some of the bundle has been used. I have one drawer for each color that includes all types of fabrics (cottons, batiks, wovens, and so on) because I use them all together. A few drawers have two colors if I don't have as many of those particular colors. For example, I have one drawer where I store both pink and purple. On the other hand, I have two drawers for blue, one for aqua, and one for other blues. Assess what you have and adjust accordingly.

Strips

After the fat quarters have been cut into, they remain in the color drawers until they become less than 6″ wide. At that point, I cut them into strips and add them to my strip bins according to size. These bins are the first place I go to when I need strips. I have a plastic portable bin with a lid for strips 1½″, 2″, 2½″, and 3½″ in width. The stored strips are folded in half with like colors. This keeps them tidy, wrinkle-free, and ready to use. If I need to make a quick block or start a project, I have strips available. It's also a great way to keep leftover strips from getting wadded up in the bottom of my scrap basket.

Chunks

Odd-shaped chunks of fabric that can't be cut into strips go into a scrap basket on my counter. This is where I look when I need a small scrap for a label or an appliqué piece. I always check here before cutting into a larger piece of fabric. Leftover charm squares and cut pieces go here. This basket gets regular sorting and shuffling, but it comes in very handy. Having it on the counter means I can't ignore it when it starts to overflow.

Bits

The bits are tiny pieces of leftover strips or chunks that are generally no larger than 3″. If you want to know how I use these, see *Wash Day* (page 61). These are great for take-along sewing and smaller projects, such as hexies and yo-yos. This little bin of bits is the last stop in my sewing stash. If it doesn't get used from here, it either gets tossed or given away. By the time it hits this bin, there's a good chance the fabric has appeared in several of my projects and I'm ready to move on to something else anyway.

The Rest

I keep a bag by the door for fabrics that no longer need to be in my sewing room. Fat quarters from a bundle that I don't plan to use, scraps that I'm tired of seeing, and even leftover backing that I have no use for all go in the bag. I take this bag to my local quilt guild meeting for the giveaway table. By giving away these fabrics, I keep my stash tidy and manageable.

CUTTING TECHNIQUES

It's time to think about the way you cut your fabric. The direction you cut your strips from the yardage, fat quarters, or even scraps makes a difference. While teaching workshops, I've seen enough quilters discover how much accuracy and ease is achieved by cutting fabric with the grain (rather than across the grain) to know it makes a difference. When there is less stretching, there is less chance for mismatched seams, less need for trimming, and less chance of puckers or tucks.

If you've ever cut border strips from the lengthwise grain of the fabric, you will know what I mean. Handling and sewing strips that don't stretch versus ones that do (cross grain) really can make the difference in a successful patchwork project. If it's easier, and results are better, you need to try it!

The following tips and photos explain *how* I cut my fabrics. Once you try it, you will understand *why*.

Fat Quarters

Once they are pressed, fat quarters are ready to use. After cutting the selvage off, the strips can continue to be cut as needed parallel to the selvage edge. This results in strips that are 18″ long and perfect for any of the quilts in this book. Cutting this way follows the grain of the fabric and prevents strips from stretching as they would if cut cross grain (perpendicular to the selvage).

1. Trim the selvage.

2. Cut strips parallel to selvage cut.

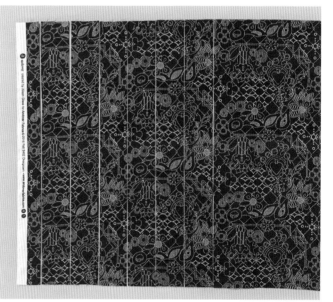

Why 18″ Strips?

Strips that are 18″ are easier to manage than longer strips. There will never be a need to use a strip any longer than 18″ for any project in this book. Cutting strips from the width of a fat quarter or a half-yard will result in 18″ strips. All patterns in this book are calculated using strips 18″ or shorter. When using scraps, if your strips are shorter than 18″, simply add more strips to compensate.

Yardage

Always cut half-yard pieces off of yardage before cutting the fabric into strips. Half-yard cuts allow for easier handling. After trimming the selvages off, cut strips from the lengthwise grain to prevent stretching of strips, resulting in better piecing and more accurate blocks. Follow the steps for cutting fat quarters when cutting half-yards into strips. Every cut from the folded fabric will result in two strips instead of one!

Cut half-yard pieces for easier handling.

STRIP SECRET
Save Your Selvages

Selvage Spools (page 65) uses selvage strips, rather than regular fabric strips, to add interest to the quilt. To build your stash of selvages for this project, leave a minimum of ¼″ of printed fabric beyond the selvage when trimming the selvage from yardage and fat quarters. Better yet, leave ½″–2″ of fabric on some selvages for variety and for more options when sewing them.

Scraps

Trimming odd size scraps into strips will help control your scrap basket. If you are unsure where the grainline on the fabric is, turn it over to the unprinted side or examine the edges to see where the threads are beginning to fray. These clues will help with cutting the fabric on the grainline. Trimming squares and strips of fabric into usable sizes will allow sorting and organized storage now, rather than chaos later. It will also keep the fabrics pressed and ready for use, rather than being wadded up in the bottom of the pile!

QUILT ASSEMBLY

Most of the quilts in this book are made by sewing the blocks into vertical rows, rather than horizontal rows as done for many traditional quilts. Refer to the quilt assembly diagrams to see examples of this. It is necessary to sew vertical rows when the rows are offset, such as in *Shimmer* (page 17). Sewing blocks into vertical rows also has the benefit of needing to use only one or two pins when hanging the row on the design wall. This makes the task of rearranging rows to audition different settings easier as well. It also allows for fewer seams to be sewn after the units are large and more difficult to manage. Also, sewing the rows into pairs before adding additional rows allows the quilter to work with smaller sections of the quilt, rather than trying to piece rows onto larger sections of the quilt, which can be cumbersome and challenging.

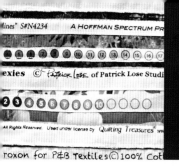

Strip Sets

Sewing strips together to create a fabric unit results in strip sets. A *strip set* is simply two or more strips sewn together lengthwise. What you do with these strip sets is where the magic happens. Creating accurate, flat, straight sets to begin with will determine how successful your patchwork results will be. While saving time and ease of sewing are important, great results are the goal.

MAKING STRIP SETS

Accurate strip sets are the result of every step along the way. Now that you've cut your strips from the lengthwise grain (parallel to the selvage), let's take a look at the sewing steps that will ensure the best results. Following these steps and avoiding issues before they arise will make the process fun and successful.

1. Mark an accurate ¼″ seam allowance on the bed of the sewing machine to ensure consistent seam allowances.

2. Rather than pinning the strips, hold the strips down with light pressure to avoid shifting of the bottom strip.

3. Always press the seams from the back side before turning over and pressing from the front side. This will allow the seams to always go in the direction intended and will help prevent distortion. Lining up strips sets on a pressing surface that has marked lines will also prevent the curving of straight seams.

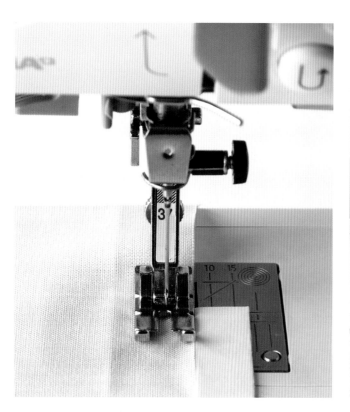

COMMON PROBLEMS TO AVOID

Curves   When strip sets are curved like rainbows, the problem is typically with the pressing. Avoid using too much pressure and line up the edge of the strip sets with a marked line on the pressing surface. If the pressing surface doesn't have lines, layer a piece of striped fabric on the pressing surface before pressing the strip sets. Always press from the back of the strip sets to ensure the seam allowances are going the desired direction. Then flip the strip set to the right side and press again.

Gaps   Be careful to ensure that the seams are completely flat when pressing them from the front. One of the most common mistakes in strip piecing is pressed strips that are not completely open at the seam. This creates issues with size and sewing in future steps.

Uneven strips   There are several ways to ensure strips on both the bottom and top feed through the sewing machine evenly. Cutting strips from the lengthwise grain is the most important step to remember. Also, keeping light pressure on the strip set with the guiding hand will help prevent shifting. If the strips are still uneven, check to make sure the bobbin tension is correct. If the tension needs adjusting it may act as a "gathering" method and strips will not finish at the proper length.

Waves   Strip sets that don't lie flat once they are pressed could be suffering from inconsistent seam allowances. Measure the seam allowances and make adjustments as needed. Marking the machine bed with washi tape will ensure consistent seam allowances. Note that not all ¼″ sewing foot attachments are created equal. Measure and mark every machine you use to ensure they are all the same ¼″.

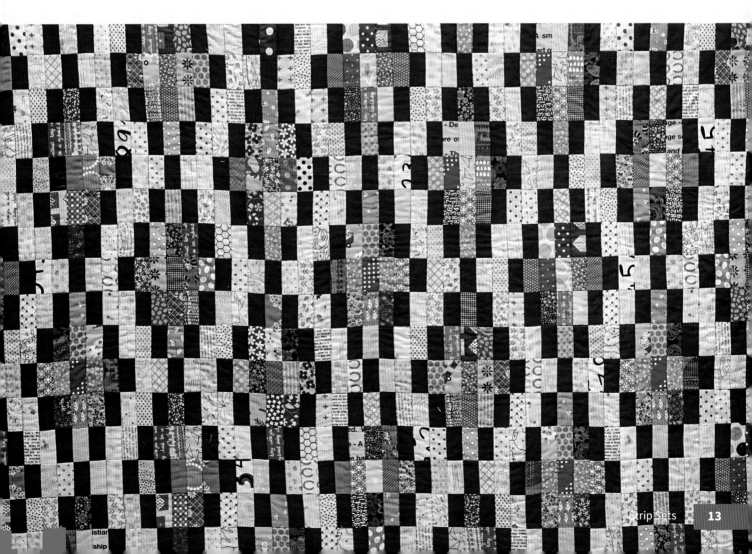

SUBCUTTING STRIP SETS

Once your strip sets are sewn and pressed, you are ready for the next step. Crosscutting or subcutting strip sets will create new units for you to sew. It's important to cut carefully following these steps so the units are the correct size and shape.

1. When layering more than one strip set for cutting, stagger them at least ¼″–½″ to distribute the bulk created by seam allowances.

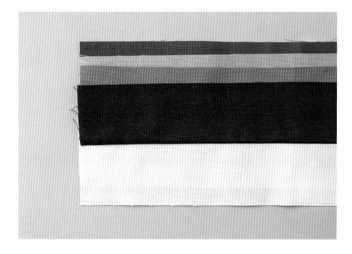

2. Trim the ends of the strip set(s) as needed.

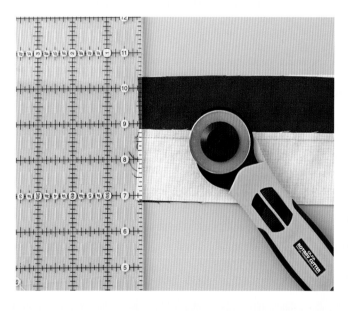

3. Always line up the guides on the ruler with the seamlines on the strips sets rather than the edges for better accuracy.

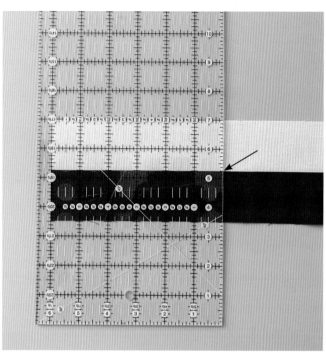

4. Measure over three sets from the left, and make the first cut here.

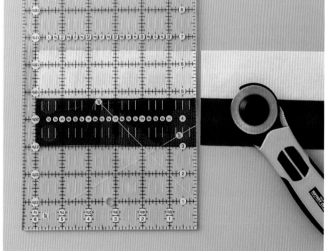

5. Measure over two sets from the left cut, and make the second cut here.

6. Finally, measure one set from the left, and make the third cut here. Working from right to left prevents the strip sets from shifting and becoming angled or slanted.

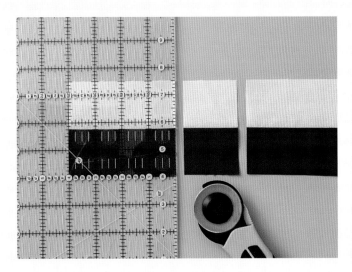

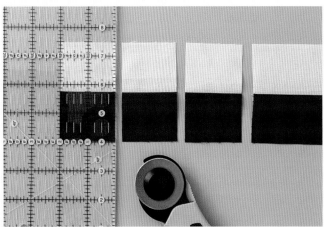

SEWING SETS TOGETHER

Once the original strip sets have been sewn and cut, it's time to arrange them and sew them back together. The following steps will provide a guide for making sure the seams line up and the seam allowances are not overlapping. Proper hand placement and pressing will help avoid problems.

1. Nest the seams.

2. Whenever possible, place the seam allowances on the top unit facing toward the needle as you feed them into the machine. This will encourage the seams to nest together rather than slip apart.

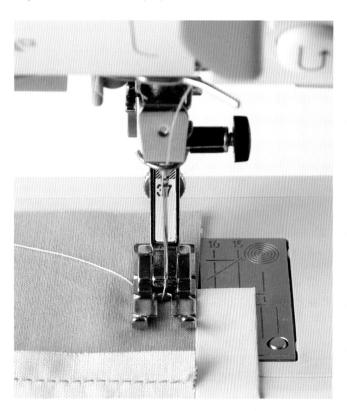

3. Place fingertips on the stitched seamlines on top to prevent the shifting of the seams and fabrics underneath.

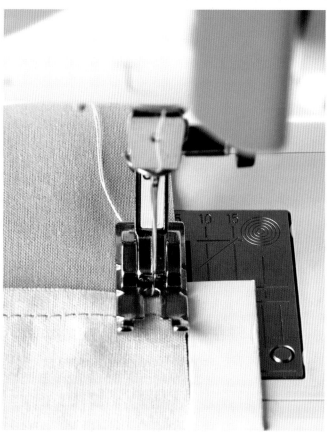

4. Check the results often and make adjustments as needed.

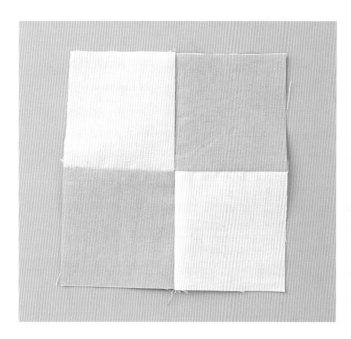

5. Pinwheel the seam allowances to distribute bulk.

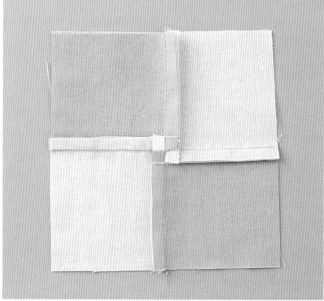

SHIMMER

FINISHED QUILT: 55″ × 72″ • **FINISHED BLOCK: 6″ × 12″**

Shimmer, 55″ × 72″, pieced and quilted by Diane D. Knott

This quilt requires 2½″ strips that are sewn together and then cut into 1½″ sections. The rectangular pieces create the elongated effect. Don't be scared by these tiny pieces; the strip sets make this quilt go much more quickly than it would seem!

MATERIALS
for Twin-Size Quilt*

Purple: 2¼ yards**

Bright prints: 2¼ yards total**

White prints: 2¼ yards total**

Backing: 3¾ yards (pieced crosswise)

Binding: ½ yard

Batting: 63″ × 80″

* See the chart Alternative Quilt Sizes (page 18) to make this quilt in crib, full/queen, or king size.

** Instead of working with yardage, you can use assorted fabrics you have and simply cut the required number of strips noted in the cutting list for each fabric.

CUTTING

Purple

• Cut 56 strips 2½″ × 18″
for strip sets.

Bright prints

• Cut 61 total strips 2½″ × 18″
for strip sets.

White prints

• Cut 56 total strips 2½″ × 18″
for strip sets.

Binding

• Cut 7 strips 2″ × width of fabric,
or use your preferred width for
binding.

ALTERNATIVE QUILT SIZES

	CRIB 49″ × 60″	FULL/QUEEN 79″ × 84″	KING 97″ × 96″
Purple	1¾ yards	3¼ yards	4¼ yards
Bright prints	1¾ yards total	3¼ yards total	4¾ yards total
White prints	2¼ yards total	3¾ yards total	4¾ yards total
Blocks (6″ × 12″)	40 blocks (8 half-blocks), arranged 8 blocks × 5 blocks	91 blocks (12 half-blocks), arranged 13 blocks × 7 blocks	128 blocks (14 half-blocks), arranged 16 blocks × 8 blocks
Backing	3¼ yards (pieced crosswise)	7¼ yards (pieced crosswise)	8¾ yards
Binding	½ yard	¾ yard	¾ yard
Batting	57″ × 68″	87″ × 92″	105″ × 104″

BLOCK ASSEMBLY

Always use a ¼″ seam allowance. • Arrows indicate the pressing direction.

Make Strip Set A

1. Sew 2 purple and 4 white strips as shown. Make 5. *Fig. A*

2. Cut each strip set into 12 units 1½″ wide. Make 60.
Set aside 6 units for side border.

Make Strip Set B

1. Sew 2 purple, 3 white, and 1 bright strip as shown. Make 9. *Fig. B*

2. Cut each strip set into 12 units 1½″ wide. Make 108.

Make Strip Set C

1. Sew 2 purple, 1 white, and 3 bright strips as shown. Make 9. *Fig. C*

2. Cut each strip set into 12 units 1½″ wide. Make 108.

Make Strip Set D

1. Sew 1 purple and 5 bright strips as shown. Make 5. *Fig. D*

2. Cut each strip set into 12 units 1½″ wide. Make 54.

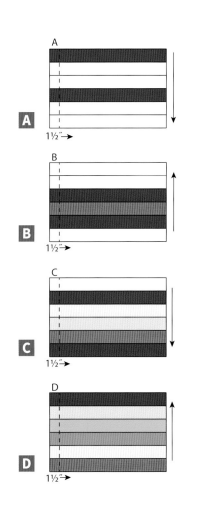

Make Blocks

1. Arrange strip sets as shown: A, B, C, D, C, and B. *Fig. E*

2. Sew the units into pairs, then sew the pairs together. Make 50. (There will be some leftover units.) *Figs. F & G*

Make Half-Blocks

1. Arrange enough cut units for 4 blocks.

2. Unsew the center horizontal seam on the cut units. *Fig. H*

3. Sew the cut units together to make half-blocks. Make 8. *Fig. I*

SIDE BORDER ASSEMBLY

Sew 6 Strip Set A units together lengthwise to make the side border strip. Make 1. *Fig. J*

QUILT ASSEMBLY

1. Arrange the blocks and half-blocks as shown. *Fig. K*

2. Sew the blocks into vertical rows.

3. Sew the rows into pairs, then sew the pairs together.

4. Sew the border strip to the right edge of the quilt.

FINISHING

Layer, baste, and quilt as desired. Bind the quilt.

TIP Try a Table Runner

Make just one row in holiday colors and create a runner to add sparkle to your table!

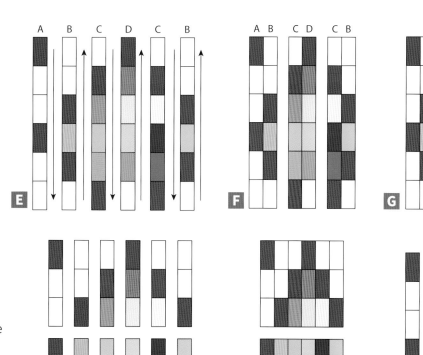

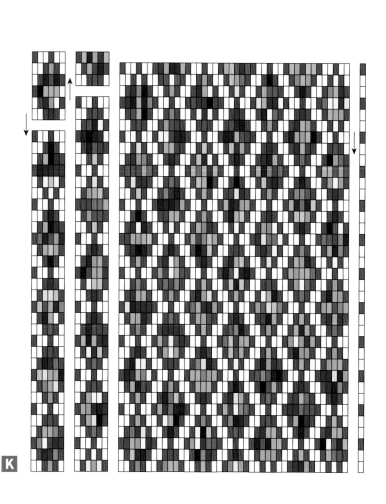

CHAIN REACTION

FINISHED QUILT: 62″ × 81″ • FINISHED BLOCK: 6″ × 11″

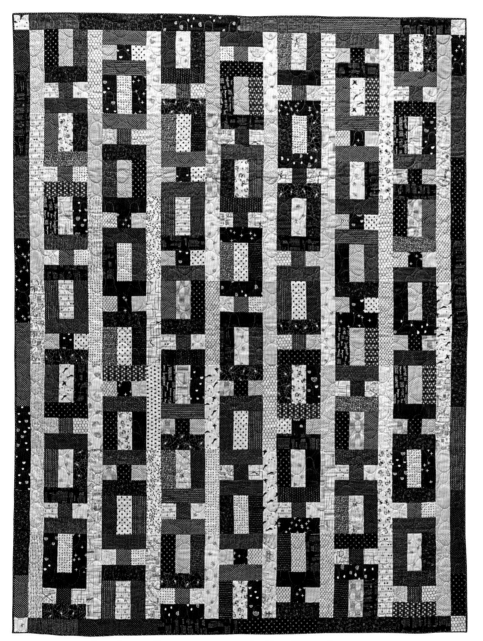

Chain Reaction, 62″ × 81″, pieced by Diane D. Knott, quilted by Millie Rondon

Black and white quilts are so fun to make! This quilt creates a chain with simple strip sets. It would be fun to make in any two-color combination.

MATERIALS
for Twin-Size Quilt*

Black prints: 3½ yards total**

White prints: 2½ yards total**

Backing: 5¼ yards

Binding: ⅝ yard

Batting: 70″ × 89″

* See the chart Alternative Quilt Sizes (next page) to make this quilt in crib, full/queen, or king size.

** Instead of working with yardage, you can use assorted fabrics you have and simply cut the required number of strips noted in the cutting list for each fabric.

CUTTING

Black prints

- Cut 34 total strips 2½″ × 18″ for Strip Set A.

- Cut 7 total strips 2½″ × 18″ for Strip Set B.

- Cut 98 total strips 2½″ × 6½″ for blocks.

- Cut 20 total strips 2½″ × 11½″ for borders.

- Cut 2 total strips 2½″ × 6″ for side borders.

- Cut 2 total strips 2½″ × 7½″ for top and bottom borders.

White prints

- Cut 17 total strips 2½″ × 18″ for Strip Set A.

- Cut 14 total strips 2½″ × 18″ for Strip Set B.

- Cut 56 total strips 2½″ × 11½″ for sashing.

- Cut 4 total squares 2½″ × 2½″ for top and bottom border corners.

Binding

- Cut 8 strips 2″ × width of fabric, or use your preferred width for binding.

ALTERNATIVE QUILT SIZES

	CRIB 54″ × 59″	FULL/QUEEN 78″ × 92″	KING 103″ × 94″
Black prints	2¼ yards total	4¼ yards total	6 yards total
White prints	1¾ yards total	3¼ yards total	4½ yards total
Blocks (6″ × 11″)	30 blocks, arranged 6 blocks × 5 blocks	72 blocks, arranged 9 blocks × 8 blocks	99 blocks, arranged 11 blocks × 9 blocks
Backing	3¾ yards	7¼ yards (pieced crosswise)	8¾ yards
Binding	½ yard	¾ yard	¾ yard
Batting	62″ × 67″	86″ × 100″	111″ × 102″

BLOCK ASSEMBLY

Always use a ¼″ seam allowance.
Arrows indicate the pressing direction.

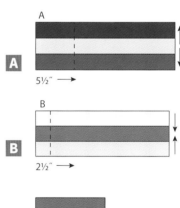

A

B

5½″ →

2½″ →

Make Strip Set A

1. Sew a 2½″ × 18″ black strip to both sides of a 2½″ × 18″ white strip. *Fig. A*

2. Make 17 strip sets.

3. Cut each strip set into 3 units 5½″ wide. Make 49.

Make Strip Set B

1. Sew a 2½″ × 18″ white strip to both sides of a 2½″ × 18″ black strip. *Fig. B*

2. Make 7 strip sets.

3. Cut each strip set into 7 units 2½″ wide. Make 49.

C

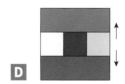

D

Make Blocks

1. Sew a 2½″ × 6½″ black strip to the sides of the Strip Set B units. Make 49. *Figs. C & D*

2. Sew this unit to a Strip Set A unit as shown. Make 49. *Fig. E*

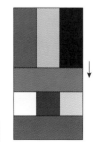

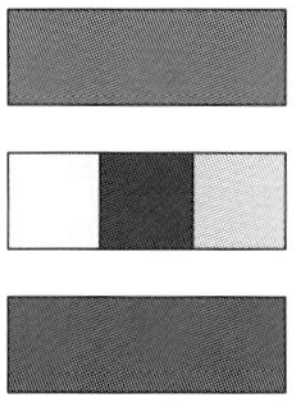

E

SASHING ASSEMBLY

Sew 7 white 2½˝ × 11½˝ strips together end to end. Make 8. *Fig. F*

BORDER ASSEMBLY

1. Sew 6 black strips 2½˝ × 11½˝ together end to end for the side borders. Make 2.

2. Sew a 2½˝ × 6˝ black strip to each end of the sewn strips. *Fig. G*

3. Sew 4 black strips 2½˝ × 11½˝ together end to end for the top and bottom borders. Make 2.

4. Sew a 2½˝ × 7½˝ black strip to each end of the sewn strips. Sew a white print corner square to the ends. *Fig. H*

QUILT ASSEMBLY

1. Arrange the blocks into 7 vertical rows. Reverse the blocks every other row. *Fig. I*

2. Sew the blocks into vertical rows.

3. Sew a sashing strip to the side of 6 rows.

4. Sew the rows with sashing into pairs, then sew the pairs together.

5. Sew sashing strips to both sides of the remaining row.

6. Join the rows.

7. Sew the side borders to the quilt.

8. Sew the top and bottom borders to the quilt.

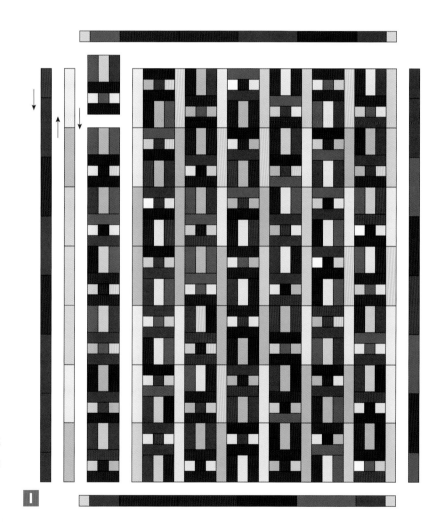

FINISHING

Layer, baste, and quilt as desired. This quilt has an oval pattern quilted that mimics the chain in the patchwork. Bind the quilt.

 Seeing in Black and White

Any quilt can be turned into a black and white quilt by simply dividing the elements into light and dark. Make a black-and-white photocopy of any quilt design to preview it before sewing.

SQUARE PEGS

FINISHED QUILT: 60″ × 78″ • FINISHED BLOCK: 9″ × 9″

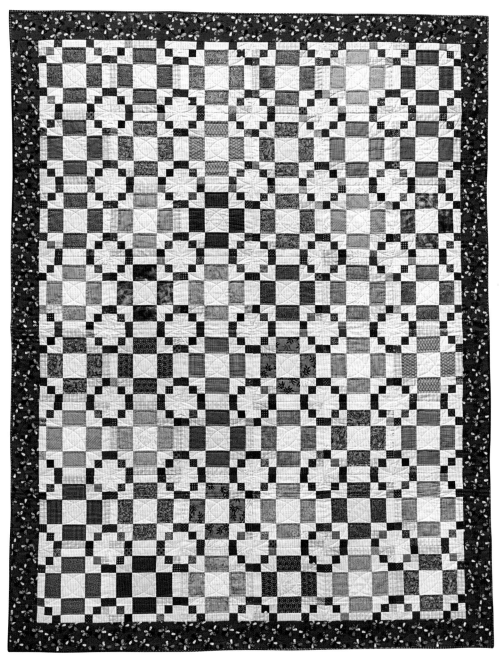

Square Pegs, 60″ × 78″, pieced and quilted by Diane D. Knott

This quilt design was inspired by a floor mat! I took a photo of the floor mat, then I spotted the same design in another location and felt it was meant to be. The secondary pattern where the blocks meet are my favorite part of this quilt design.

MATERIALS
for Twin-Size Quilt*

Aqua prints: 1¾ yards total**

Red, brown, and aqua prints: 1½ yards total**

Cream prints: 3¾ yards total**

Red: 2¼ yards for borders

Backing: 5 yards

Binding: ⅝ yard

Batting: 68″ × 86″

* See the chart Alternative Quilt Sizes (page 24) to make this quilt in crib, full/queen, or king size.

** Instead of working with yardage, you can use assorted fabrics you have and simply cut the required number of strips noted in the cutting list for each fabric.

CUTTING

Aqua prints

• Cut 48 total strips 2½″ × 15″ for Strip Set A.

Red, brown, and aqua prints

• Cut 48 total strips 1½″ × 18″ for Strip Sets B and C.

Cream prints

• Cut 48 total strips 1½″ × 15″ for Strip Set A.

• Cut 32 total strips 2½″ × 18″ for Strip Set B.

• Cut 32 total strips 1½″ × 18″ for Strip Set C.

• Cut 10 total strips 3½″ × 18″. Subcut strips into 48 squares 3½″ × 3½″ for blocks.

Red

• Cut 2 strips 3½″ × 72½″ for side borders.

• Cut 2 strips 3½″ × 60½″ for top and bottom borders.

Binding

• Cut 8 strips 2″ × width of fabric, or your preferred width for binding.

ALTERNATIVE QUILT SIZES

	CRIB 51″ × 60″	FULL/QUEEN 87″ × 87″	KING 105″ × 105″
Aqua prints	1 yard total	2½ yards total	3¾ yards total
Red, brown, and aqua prints	1¼ yards total	2¼ yards total	2¾ yards total
Cream prints	2¼ yards total	5¼ yards total	7 yards total
Red	1¾ yards	2½ yards	3 yards
Blocks (9″ × 9″)	30 blocks, arranged 5 blocks × 6 blocks	81 blocks, arranged 9 blocks × 9 blocks	121 blocks, arranged 11 blocks × 11 blocks
Backing	3½ yards (pieced crosswise)	8 yards	9½ yards
Binding	½ yard	¾ yard	¾ yard
Batting	59″ × 68″	95″ × 95″	113″ × 113″

BLOCK ASSEMBLY

Always use a ¼″ seam allowance.
Arrows indicate the pressing direction.

Make Strip Set A

1. Sew a 1½″ × 15″ cream strip to a 2½″ × 15″ aqua strip. Make 48.

2. Cut each strip set into 4 units 3½″ wide. *Fig. A*

3. Keep the sets of 4 matching pieces together.

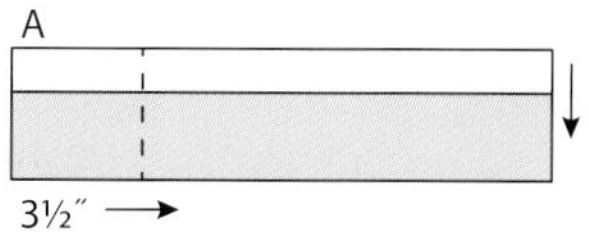

Make Strip Set B

1. Sew a 1½″ × 18″ red, brown, or aqua strip to a 2½″ × 18″ cream strip. Make 32.

2. Cut each strip set into 12 units 1½″ wide. Make 384. *Fig. B*

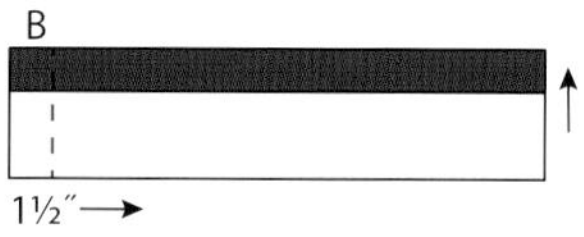

Make Strip Set C

1. Sew a 1½″ × 18″ cream strip to both sides of a 1½″ × 18″ red, brown, or aqua strip. Make 16.

2. Cut each strip set into 12 units 1½″ wide. Make 192. *Fig. C*

Make Corner Units

Sew 2 units from Strip Set B to the sides of 1 unit from Strip Set C. Make 96 and 96 reversed. *Figs. D–F*

Make Blocks

1. Arrange 4 corner units with 4 units from Strip Set A and 1 cream 3½″ × 3½″ square as shown. Sew 3 rows of 3 units. *Fig. G*

2. Sew the rows together. Make 48. *Fig. H*

QUILT ASSEMBLY

1. Sew 6 vertical rows of 8 blocks each.

2. Sew the rows together.

3. Sew the 3½″ × 72½″ border strips to the sides of the quilt.

4. Sew the 3½″ × 60½″ border strips to the top and bottom of the quilt. *Fig. I*

FINISHING

Layer, baste, and quilt as desired. This quilt features free-motion machine quilting using curved rulers as a guide; an overall design would work as well. Bind the quilt.

STRIP SECRET
Make a Scrappy Binding

Did you notice the scrappy binding on this quilt? It is made from the brown fabrics found in the quilt. Consider using leftover strips for binding rather than cutting a new fabric.

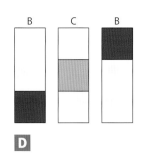

B   C   B

D

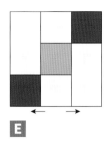

E

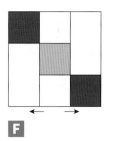

F

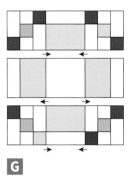

G

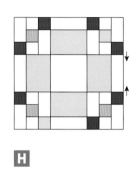

H

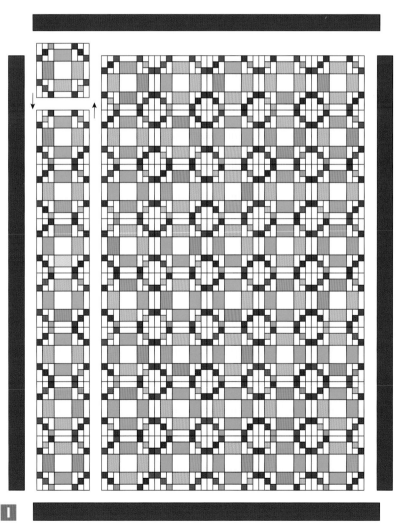

I

Triangles from Strips

Discovering that triangles could be cut from strips changed the way I make triangles forever. No more over-sizing squares, no more marking lines, and no more trimming slivers! Simply cut the triangles needed from the strips you already have, and you are done! There's only one tiny triangle of seam allowance to trim away. What's not to love about making triangles more accurately and more easily? This method is the only one I use.

MAKING TRIANGLES FROM STRIPS

Once the fabric is cut into strips, cutting other shapes from those strips becomes very easy. Use a 45° ruler with a flat edge or grayed-out triangle at the tip to cut triangles from the strips such as the fast2cut Bonnie K. Hunter's Essential Triangle Tool (from C&T Publishing). Using the 45° line on a regular ruler will result in triangles that are too small.

1. Layer the strips right sides together.

2. Trim the ends.

3. Make the first cut with the 45° triangle ruler.

4. Rotate the ruler for the next cut and repeat.

  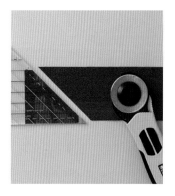 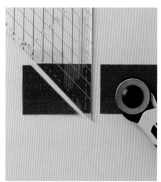

MAKING HALF-SQUARE TRIANGLES FROM STRIPS

When the fabrics are cut as shown above, they will be ready to sew without pinning. This simple method for half-square triangles results in no over-sizing or trimming. No waste, no mess, and perfect results every time!

1. Sew ¼″ from the longest side of the triangle.

2. Press the seams toward the dark fabric, from the back first, then flip to the front and press again.

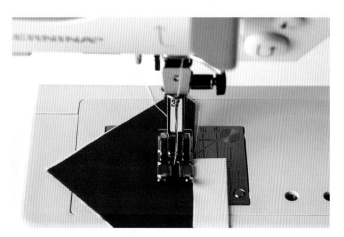 

SPLASH

FINISHED QUILT: 46″ × 58″ • FINISHED BLOCK: 10″ × 10″

Splash, 46″ × 58″, pieced and quilted by Diane D. Knott

The first version of this quilt was made using my dad's blue plaid shirts and a white background. It was given to my mom as a remembrance quilt. This version uses batik prints, but the first version will always be special to me.

MATERIALS
for Crib-Size Quilt*

Bright prints:
2¼ yards total**

Background: 3 yards

Backing: 3 yards
(pieced crosswise)

Binding: ½ yard

Batting: 54″ × 66″

* See the chart Alternative Quilt Sizes (page 28) to make this quilt in twin, full/queen, or king size.

** Instead of working with yardage, you can use assorted fabrics you have and simply cut the required number of strips noted in the cutting list for each fabric.

CUTTING

Bright prints

- Cut 4 matching squares 2½″ × 2½″ and 3 strips 2½″ × 18″ for each of 12 blocks.

- Cut 62 total squares 2½″ × 2½″ for sashing.

- Cut 2 total strips 2½″ × 15″ for border corner blocks.

Background

Note: Cut border strips first.

- Cut 2 strips 4½″ × 50½″ for side borders.

- Cut 2 strips 4½″ × 38½″ for top and bottom borders.

- Cut 36 strips 2½″ × 18″ for blocks.

- Cut 80 squares 2½″ × 2½″ for blocks and cornerstones.

- Cut 31 strips 2½″ × 6½″ for sashing.

- Cut 2 strips 2½″ × 15″ for border corner blocks.

Binding

- Cut 6 strips 2″ × width of fabric, or use your preferred width for binding.

ALTERNATIVE QUILT SIZES

	TWIN 58″ × 70″	FULL/QUEEN 82″ × 82″	KING 94″ × 94″
Bright prints	3 yards total	5½ yards total	7 yards total
Background	3¾ yards	6¾ yards	8¾ yards
Blocks (10″ × 10″)	20 blocks, arranged 4 blocks × 5 blocks	36 blocks, arranged 6 blocks × 6 blocks	49 blocks, arranged 7 blocks × 7 blocks
Backing	4½ yards	7¾ yards	9¼ yards
Binding	½ yard	¾ yard	¾ yard
Batting	66″ × 78″	90″ × 90″	102″ × 102″

BLOCK ASSEMBLY

Always use a ¼″ seam allowance. Arrows indicate the pressing direction.

1. Layer 3 bright strips and 3 background strips right sides together. Make 16 half-square triangles (see Making Half-Square Triangles from Strips, page 26).

2. Arrange 4 bright squares, 5 background squares, and the 16 half-square triangles as shown. *Fig. A*

3. Sew the units into rows. Sew the rows together. Make 12 blocks. *Fig. B*

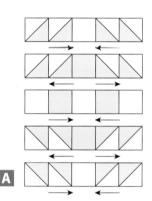

A

SASHING ASSEMBLY

Sew a 2½″ × 2½″ bright square to the ends of a 2½″ × 6½″ background sashing strip. Make 31. *Fig. C*

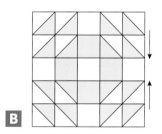

B

C

BORDER CORNER BLOCK ASSEMBLY

1. Layer 2 bright strips and 2 background strips right sides together. Make 16 half-square triangles.

2. Sew 2 sets of half-square triangles together as shown. *Fig. D*

3. Sew sets into a square. Make 4 border corner blocks. *Fig. E*

QUILT ASSEMBLY

1. Sew the sashing units and cornerstone squares into 4 vertical rows as shown.

2. Alternate 4 blocks and 5 sashing units and sew into vertical rows as shown.

3. Sew the block rows and sashing rows together.

4. Sew the 4½″ × 50½″ borders to the sides of the quilt.

5. Sew a corner border block onto each end of the 4½″ × 38½″ borders.

6. Sew the borders with the corner blocks to the top and bottom of the quilt. *Fig. F*

FINISHING

Layer, baste, and quilt as desired. This quilt features free-motion machine quilting; any overall design would work as well. Bind the quilt.

 **Cut Ahead**

Cut all the elements needed for each block and have them ready to go. Use a binder clip for each block to keep the pieces together. If you only have a few minutes to sew, you'll be able to stitch up a block or two in a flash.

AUNT ELSIE

FINISHED QUILT: 50″ × 70″ • FINISHED BLOCK: 10″ × 10″

Aunt Elsie, 50″ × 70″, pieced and quilted by Diane D. Knott

My great-aunt Elsie was considered an old maid in her time. She was the loveliest and sweetest woman I ever met. These fabrics reminded me of her homemade skirts and aprons that she always wore. Alternating the light and dark fabrics in these blocks creates a simple grid setting.

MATERIALS FOR TWIN-SIZE QUILT*

Bright prints: 2¾ yards total*

Background prints: 2¾ yards total*

Backing: 3¼ yards (pieced crosswise)

Binding: ½ yard

Batting: 58″ × 78″

* See the chart Alternative Quilt Sizes (next page) to make this quilt in crib, full/queen, or king size.

** Instead of working with yardage, you can use assorted fabrics you have and simply cut the required number of strips noted in the cutting list for each fabric.

CUTTING

Bright prints

- Cut 2 matching strips 2½″ × 18″ for each of 35 blocks.

Background prints

- Cut 2 matching strips 2½″ × 18″ for each of 35 blocks.

Binding

- Cut 7 strips 2″ × width of fabric, or use your preferred width for binding.

ALTERNATIVE QUILT SIZES

	CRIB: 40″ × 60″	FULL/QUEEN: 80″ × 80″	KING: 100″ × 90″
Bright prints	1¾ yards	4¼ yards	6¼ yards
Background prints	1¾ yards	4¼ yards	6¼ yards
Blocks (10″ × 10″)	24 blocks, arranged 4 blocks × 6 blocks	64 blocks, arranged 8 blocks × 8 blocks	90 blocks, arranged 10 blocks × 9 blocks
Backing	2¾ yards (pieced crosswise)	7½ yards	8¼ yards (pieced crosswise)
Binding	½ yard	¾ yard	¾ yard
Batting	48″ × 68	88″ × 88″	108″ × 98″

BLOCK ASSEMBLY

Always use a ¼″ seam allowance.
Arrows indicate the pressing direction.

1. Layer 1 bright strip and 1 background strip right sides together. Make 8 half-square triangles (see Making Half-Square Triangles from Strips, page 26).

2. From the remaining bright strips, cut 9 squares 2½″ × 2½″.

3. From the remaining background strips, cut 8 squares 2½″ × 2½″.

4. Arrange the half-square triangles and the squares in rows as shown. *Fig. A*

5. Sew the rows together. Make 18 blocks. *Fig. B*

6. Reverse the bright fabric and background fabric placement. Make 17 blocks. *Fig. C*

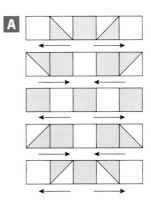

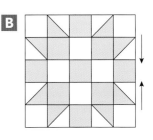

QUILT ASSEMBLY

1. Sew the blocks into 5 vertical rows of 7 blocks each, alternating light and dark blocks as shown. *Fig. D*

2. Sew the rows into pairs, then sew the pairs of rows together. Add the remaining row.

FINISHING

Layer, baste, and quilt as desired. This quilt features machine quilting in an overall clamshell design. Any curved quilting pattern would complement the straight lines of the patchwork. Bind the quilt.

STRIP SECRET
Use Precut Strip Bundles

This pattern is perfect for using precut 2½˝ strips!

D

FIESTA

FINISHED QUILT: 53½″ × 64½″ • FINISHED BLOCK: 5½″ × 5½″

Fiesta, 53½″ × 64½″, pieced and quilted by Diane D. Knott

The color palette for this quilt was based on a fun fabric I fell in love with. I dove into my strip bins and found everything I needed. This quilt was so cheerful and busy that I simply quilted in the ditch.

MATERIALS
for Crib-Size Quilt*

Light prints:
2¾ yards total**

Dark prints: 3 yards total**

Backing: 3½ yards
(pieced crosswise)

Binding: ½ yard

Batting: 61″ × 72″

* See the chart Alternative Quilt Sizes (page 34) to make this quilt in twin, full/queen, or king size.

** Instead of working with yardage, you can use assorted fabrics you have and simply cut the required number of strips noted in the cutting list for each fabric.

CUTTING

Light prints

- Cut 33 total strips 1½″ × 18″ for small four-patches.

- Cut 15 total strips 2½″ × 15″. Subcut each into 3 sets of 2 matching squares 2½″ × 2½″ for double four-patches.

- Cut 44 total strips 3½″ × 10″ for triangles.

- Cut 40 total sets of 2 matching squares 2½″ × 2½″ for border blocks.

Dark prints

- Cut 33 total strips 1½″ × 18″ for small four-patches.

- Cut 19 total strips 2½″ × 15″. Subcut each into 3 sets of 2 matching squares 2½″ × 2½″ for double four-patches.

- Cut 55 total strips 3½″ × 10″ for triangles.

- Cut 40 total strips 2½″ × 6″ for border blocks.

- Cut 4 total squares 2½″ × 2½″ for border corners.

Binding

- Cut 7 strips 2″ × width of fabric, or your preferred width for binding.

ALTERNATIVE QUILT SIZES

	TWIN 64½″ × 81″	FULL/QUEEN 86½″ × 86½″	KING 108½″ × 97½″
Light prints	4½ yards	6½ yards	9½ yards
Dark prints	4¾ yards	7½ yards	10¾ yards
Blocks (5½″ × 5½″)	70 light and 84 dark blocks, arranged 11 blocks × 14 blocks	105 light and 120 dark blocks, arranged 15 blocks × 15 blocks	153 light and 170 dark blocks, arranged 19 blocks × 17 blocks
Backing	5 yards	8 yards	9 yards
Binding	½ yard	¾ yard	¾ yard
Batting	72″ × 89″	94″ × 94″	116″ × 105″

BLOCK ASSEMBLY

Always use a ¼″ seam allowance. • Arrows indicate the pressing direction. Pinwheel press the four-patch seams.

Make Four-Patches

1. Sew a light 1½″ × 18″ strip to a dark 1½″ × 18″ strip.

2. Cut each strip set into 12 units 1½″ wide.

3. Layer the units right sides together and sew into four-patches. Make 99 sets of 2 matching four-patches. *Fig. A*

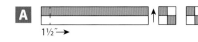

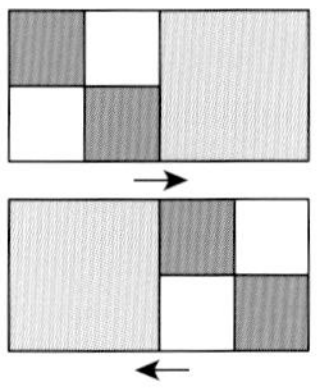

Make Double Four-Patches

1. Arrange 2 matching four-patches and 2 matching 2½″ × 2½″ light squares together as shown.

2. Sew a square to each four-patch. *Fig. B*

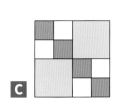

3. Sew the units together. Make 44 double four-patches with light squares. *Fig. C*

4. Repeat using matching sets of 2½″ × 2½″ dark squares. Make 55 double four-patches with dark squares. *Fig. D*

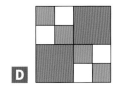

Add Setting Triangles

1. Make 4 sets of triangles from each of the 44 light 3½″ × 10″ strips (see Making Triangles from Strips, page 26).

2. Make 4 sets of triangles from each of the 55 dark 3½″ × 10″ strips.

3. Sew a light triangle to opposite sides of the light double four-patch block. *Fig. E*

4. Sew a light triangle to the remaining sides of the block. *Fig. F*

5. Trim the block to 6″. Make 44 light blocks and 55 dark blocks.

Make Border Blocks

1. Place matching light 2½″ × 2½″ squares on each end of a 6″ × 2½″ border strip.

2. Mark diagonal lines from corner to corner on the squares as shown. *Fig. G*

3. Sew on the drawn lines and trim away the excess. Make 40. *Fig. H*

QUILT ASSEMBLY

1. Sew the light blocks into 4 vertical rows of 11 blocks.

2. Sew the dark blocks into 5 vertical rows of 11 blocks.

3. Sew 1 dark row to 1 light row. Repeat. Sew the pairs together as shown. Add the last dark row.

4. Sew 11 border blocks together for each side border. Sew to the sides of the quilt.

5. Sew 9 border blocks together for each top and bottom border. Sew the corner blocks to the ends of the borders.

6. Sew to the top and bottom of the quilt. *Fig. I*

FINISHING

Layer, baste, and quilt as desired. Bind the quilt.

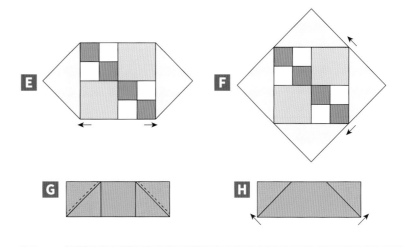

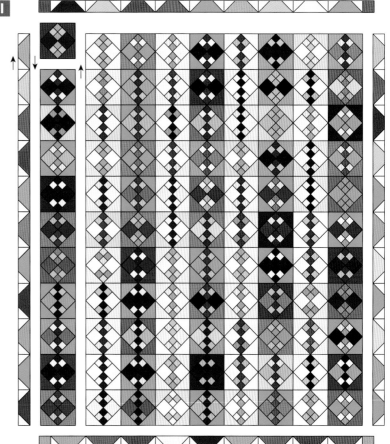

STRIP SECRET
Picking Palettes

Choose a colorful fabric as an inspiration and select shades from that fabric for the blocks. This palette will help the blocks connect with one another even if the individual blocks have different fabrics. It's not necessary to include the inspiration fabric; in this case, I used it as a backing.

Backing fabric used as inspiration for color palette

Resewing Strip Sets

Sewing strip set units together in creative ways is what I call "resewing." *One-Way Ticket* (next page) is an example of a single strip set manipulated into a fun block by cutting, unsewing, and resewing. *Lime Twist* (page 40) is a perfect example of making strips sets, cutting them, then twisting them before resewing them into blocks that use lots of strips but are very easy to assemble. *Vortex* (page 43) uses a different approach to resewing by cutting the strip sets at an angle and letting them spin around a center square. These methods take strip sets a step further.

Detail of *One-Way Ticket*

Detail of *Lime Twist*

Detail of *Vortex*

ONE-WAY TICKET

FINISHED QUILT: 60″ × 83″ • FINISHED BLOCK: 12″ × 12″

One-Way Ticket, 60″ × 83″, pieced and quilted by Diane D. Knott

This quilt is a great strip bin buster. I have made several versions of this over the years and am always surprised how differently each one turns out. These blocks all face the same direction; try turning the blocks to discover multiple designs!

MATERIALS
for Twin-Size Quilt*

White prints: 1¼ yards total**

Blue prints: 1¼ yards total**

Light pink prints: 1¼ yards total**

Black prints: 1¼ yards total**

Yellow prints: 1¼ yards total**

Green prints: 1¼ yards total**

Purple prints: 1¼ yards total**

Dark pink prints: 1¼ yards total**

Inner border: 1 fat quarter

Outer border: 2 yards

Backing: 5¼ yards

Binding: ⅝ yard

Batting: 68″ × 91″

* See the chart Alternative Quilt Sizes (page 38) to make this quilt in crib, full/queen, or king size.

** Instead of working with yardage, you can use assorted fabrics you have and simply cut the required number of strips noted in the cutting list for each fabric.

CUTTING

Prints

• Cut 25 total strips 2″ × 18″ total from each color.

Inner border

• Cut 8 strips 2″ × 18″.

Outer border

• Cut 2 strips 10½″ × 60½″.

Binding

• Cut 8 strips 2″ × width of fabric, or use your preferred width for binding.

ALTERNATIVE QUILT SIZES

	CRIB 48″ × 60″	FULL/QUEEN 84″ × 83″	KING 107″ × 96″
Each color	¾ yard	1¼ yards	1¾ yards
Inner border	(omit borders)	½ yard	½ yard
Outer border	(omit borders)	2½ yards	3 yards
Blocks **(12″ × 12″)**	20 blocks, arranged 4 blocks × 5 blocks	35 blocks, arranged 7 blocks × 5 blocks	56 blocks, arranged 8 blocks × 7 blocks
Backing	3¼ yards (pieced crosswise)	7¾ yards	8¾ yards (pieced crosswise)
Binding	½ yard	¾ yard	¾ yard
Batting	56″ × 68″	92″ × 91″	115″ × 104″

BLOCK ASSEMBLY

Always use a ¼″ seam allowance. Arrows indicate the pressing direction.

1. Arrange the strips in the preferred color order. Keep this same arrangement for all the blocks.

2. Sew 8 strips together lengthwise. Make 25. *Fig. A*

3. Sew the first and last strips lengthwise to create a tube. *Fig. B*

4. Cut the tube every 2″ to create 8 units. *Fig. C*

5. Unsew each tube at one seam as shown. Start with one color, moving to the next color on the next tube.

6. Press the seams as shown so they will nest. *Fig. D*

7. Sew the units together, creating the diagonal pattern. Make 25. *Fig. E*

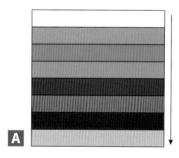

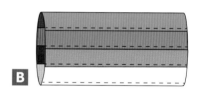

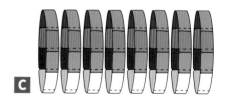

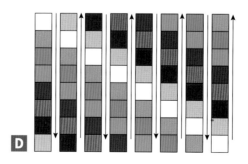

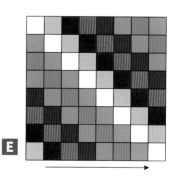

QUILT ASSEMBLY

1. Sew the blocks into 5 rows of 5 blocks each.

2. Sew the rows together.

3. Sew 4 strips end to end to create each inner border. Trim the strip to 60½″. Make 2.

4. Sew 1 inner border strip to 1 outer border strip. Make 2.

5. Sew the borders to the top and bottom of the quilt. *Fig. F*

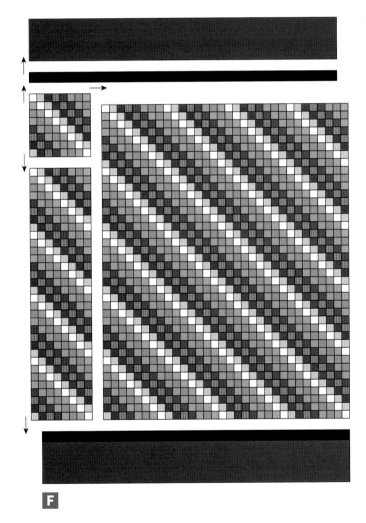

F

FINISHING

Layer, baste, and quilt as desired. This quilt features machine quilting in straight lines on the diagonal. Bind the quilt.

TIP Size It Up or Down

Skip the borders and this becomes a perfect lap-size quilt for snuggling, or add side borders to make this quilt queen-size.

I often use a strip of blocks to make the backing long enough and to prevent having to buy more fabric for the backing. These particular blocks were made on a retreat using a travel machine, and my seam allowance was different, so the blocks turned out a different size. Rather than toss them, I used them in the backing.

STRIP SECRET
Setting Surprises

These blocks have as many setting possibilities as Log Cabin blocks. By twisting and turning these blocks, many different design options are available. Play with them to find one you like.

LIME TWIST

FINISHED QUILT: 58″ × 74″ • FINISHED BLOCK: 8″ × 8″

Lime Twist, 58″ × 74″, pieced and quilted by Diane D. Knott

After years of collecting dotted print fabrics, I needed a way to play with them. This design will work with any fabric collection. Each strip set creates two blocks plus a border section, so this quilt will be finished before you can blink!

MATERIALS
for Twin-Size Quilt*

Assorted dotted prints:
24 fat quarters

Lime: 1½ yards

Backing: 4¾ yards

Binding: ½ yard

Batting: 66″ × 82″

* See the chart Alternative Quilt Sizes (next page) to make this quilt in crib, full/queen, or king size.

CUTTING

Assorted dotted prints

- Cut 18″-long strips in a variety of the following widths: 1″, 1¼″, 1½″, 1¾″, 2″, 2¼″, and 2½″. (The number of strips will vary, depending on the combination of sizes used.)

Lime

- Cut 2 strips 13″ × width of fabric. Subcut into 48 strips 1½″ × 13″ for blocks.

- Cut 6 strips 1½″ × width of fabric for inner border.

Binding

- Cut 7 strips 2″ × width of fabric, or use your preferred width for binding.

ALTERNATIVE QUILT SIZES

	CRIB 42″ × 58″	FULL/QUEEN 82″ × 82″	KING 98″ × 98″
Assorted dotted prints	12 fat quarters	42 fat quarters	61 fat quarters
Lime	¾ yard	2 yards	2½ yards
Blocks (8″ × 8″)	24 blocks, arranged 4 blocks × 6 blocks	81 blocks, arranged 9 blocks × 9 blocks	121 blocks, arranged 11 blocks × 11 blocks
Backing	3 yards (pieced crosswise)	7½ yards	9 yards
Binding	½ yard	¾ yard	¾ yard
Batting	50″ × 66″	90″ × 90″	106″ × 106″

BLOCK ASSEMBLY

Always use a ¼″ seam allowance. • Arrows indicate the pressing direction.

Make Strip Sets

1. Sew strips together in various combinations of fabrics and widths. *Fig. A*

2. Continue sewing strips until the strip set is at least 12½″ wide. If the strip set is too wide, trim it to 12½″ wide. Make 24 strip sets 12½″ × 18″.

Make Blocks

1. Trim the edge of the strip set as needed.

2. Cut a 4½″ unit for the outer border.

3. Cut a 12½″ square from the remaining piece for the blocks. *Fig. B*

4. Cut the square diagonally from corner to corner in both directions to make 4 triangles. *Fig. C*

5. Arrange the triangles as shown. Note that the strips in the triangles do *not* match; 1 triangle has lengthwise strips and the other has crosswise strips. Sew a lime strip 1½″ × 13″ between the 2 triangles. *Fig. D*

6. Trim the block to 8½″ square. Make 48 blocks. *Fig. E*

A

B

C

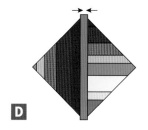

D

E

BORDER ASSEMBLY

Make Inner Borders

1. Sew the lime strips 1½″ × width of fabric together end to end.

2. Cut 2 borders 64½″ for the side borders.

3. Cut 2 borders 50½″ for the top and bottom borders.

Make Outer Borders

1. Arrange the border sections as shown.

2. Use 5 sections each for the top and bottom borders. Trim to 4½″ × 50½″.

3. Use 7 sections each for the side borders. Trim to 4½″ × 74½″. *Fig. F*

QUILT ASSEMBLY

1. Sew the blocks into 6 rows of 8 blocks each.

2. Sew the rows into pairs. Sew the pairs together.

3. Sew the lime 64½″ inner borders to the sides of the quilt.

4. Sew the lime 50½″ inner borders to the top and bottom of the quilt.

5. Sew the pieced 58½″ outer borders to the top and bottom of the quilt.

6. Sew the pieced 74½″ outer borders to the sides of the quilt. *Fig. G*

FINISHING

Layer, baste, and quilt as desired. This quilt has an overall free-motion quilting pattern. Bind the quilt.

STRIP SECRET
Pick a Theme

Choose a fat quarter bundle, holiday theme, or color combo and make this quilt to celebrate any occasion!

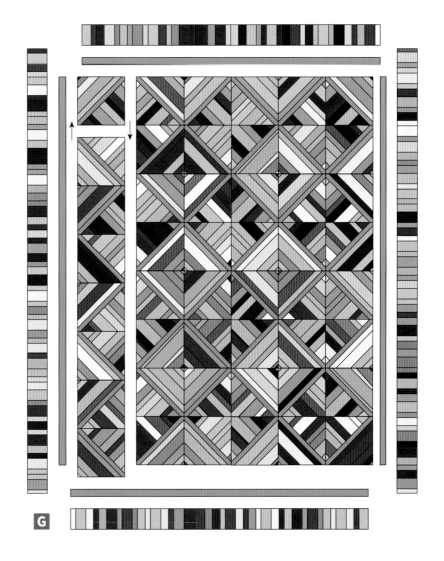

VORTEX

FINISHED QUILT: 60″ × 60″ • FINISHED BLOCK: 9″ × 9″

Vortex, 60″ × 60″, pieced by Diane D. Knott, quilted by Millie Rondon

After spying a similar version of this in a pink and white antique quilt, I knew I wanted to make my own. The construction of this quilt includes partial seams. Partial seams are used to avoid inset seams. Rather than trying to sew into the corner of seam intersections, simply leaving the seam open in the beginning and sewing it closed later creates a perfect seam intersection without any of the stress.

MATERIALS for Crib-Size Quilt*

Assorted prints: 3¼ yards total**

Black print: 1¾ yards

Yellow: 1¾ yards

Backing: 4 yards

Binding: ½ yard

Batting: 68″ × 68″

* See the chart Alternative Quilt Sizes (page 44) to make this quilt in twin, full/queen, or king size.

** Instead of working with yardage, you can use assorted fabrics you have and simply cut the required number of strips noted in the cutting list for each fabric.

CUTTING

Assorted prints

• Cut 102 total strips 2″ × 18″.

Black print

Note: Cut the border strips first.

• Cut 2 strips 2″ × 51½″
  for inner borders.

• Cut 2 border strips 2″ × 54½″
  for inner borders.

• Cut 16 squares 2″ × 2″
  for cornerstones.

• Cut 29 squares 3½″ × 3½″ for block
  centers and outer border corners.

Yellow

Note: Cut the borders first.

• Cut 4 strips 3½″ × 54½″
  for outer borders.

• Cut 40 strips 2″ × 9½″ for sashing.

Binding

• Cut 7 strips 2″ × width of fabric, or
  use your preferred width for binding.

ALTERNATIVE QUILT SIZES

	TWIN 60″ × 70½″	FULL/QUEEN 81″ × 81″	KING 102″ × 91½″
Assorted prints	3½ yards total	5½ yards total	8 yards total
Black print	2 yards	2½ yards	3 yards
Yellow	2¼ yards	2½ yards	3 yards
Blocks (9″ × 9″)	30 blocks, arranged 5 blocks × 6 blocks	49 blocks, arranged 7 blocks × 7 blocks	72 blocks, arranged 9 blocks × 8 blocks
Backing	4½ yards	7½ yards	8¼ yards (pieced crosswise)
Binding	½ yard	¾ yard	¾ yard
Batting	68″ × 78″	89″ × 89″	110″ × 99″

BLOCK ASSEMBLY

Always use a ¼″ seam allowance. • Arrows indicate the pressing direction.

Make Strip Sets

1. Sew 6 strips together lengthwise. Use different fabric combinations in each strip set. Make 17. *Fig. A*

2. Cut the strip sets into 6″ units.

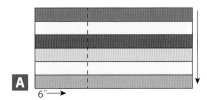

3. Cut the 6″ units on the diagonal, from corner to corner in the same direction as shown. Each strip set will yield 6 triangles. *Fig. B*

4. Make 102 triangles. (There will be 2 extra.)

Make Blocks

1. Arrange 4 triangles and 1 black 3½″ × 3½″ center square as shown. Mix and match the strip set triangles so that they are not repeated in a block. *Fig. C*

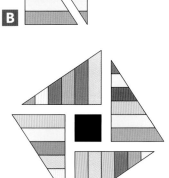

2. Sew the center square to the first triangle, sewing a 1″ partial seam. *Figs. D–G*

3. Sew the next 3 triangles according to the diagrams. *Figs. H & I*

4. Finish sewing the partial seam.

5. Trim the block to 9½″ × 9½″. Make 25.

QUILT ASSEMBLY

1. Arrange the blocks, sashing, and cornerstones as shown.

2. Sew the blocks and sashing strips into 5 rows of 5 blocks and 4 sashing strips.

3. Sew the sashing and cornerstone squares into 4 rows of 5 sashing strips and 4 cornerstones.

4. Sew a sashing row to each block row.

5. Sew the rows together.

6. Sew the 51½″ inner borders to the sides of the quilt.

7. Sew the 54½″ inner borders to the top and bottom of the quilt.

8. Sew the outer borders to the sides of the quilt.

9. Sew a 3½″ corner square to the ends of the 2 remaining outer borders.

10. Sew the outer borders to the top and bottom of the quilt. *Fig. J*

FINISHING

Layer, baste, and quilt as desired. Choose a swirling quilt design to match the swirling patchwork blocks. Bind the quilt.

 Stabilize the Edges

To stabilize the bias edges created by the diagonal cuts, mark the cutting line first, then sew a stabilizing basting stitch ⅛″ along each side before cutting. This will prevent the bias edges from stretching. Or simply baste around the edge of the block once it is assembled.

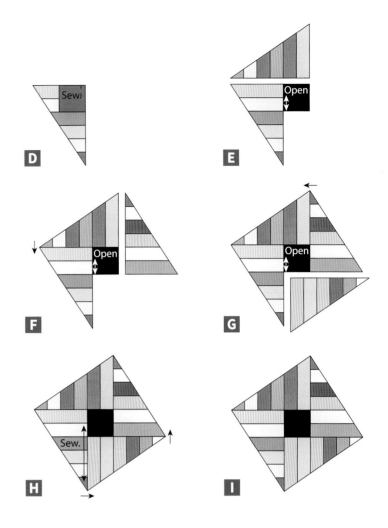

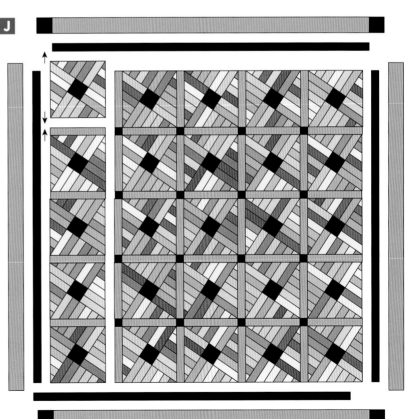

Individual Strips

Not every quilt made with strips needs a clever technique or strip sets to make it sparkle. My favorite blocks to make use individual strips added one at a time. While this method takes a bit longer, the results are worth the time invested. There are some good methods and tricks to making individual strips sew together perfectly and easily. Following these tips will prevent the typical pitfalls of sewing individual strips.

PIECING INDIVIDUAL STRIPS

When sewing individual strips into a block, such as a Log Cabin block, it's best to cut these strips to the exact length needed. This will allow you to see if your seam allowances need to be adjusted. Simply sewing a strip, then trimming it to the length of the block could result with a block that is not the desired size. Remember, small variations in seam allowance can add up quickly when repeated multiple times.

1. Layer strips right sides together along the ¼″ taped markings.

2. Keep light pressure on the strips with fingertips to prevent shifting.

4. Press the seams on the front.

3. Press the seams on the back.

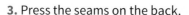

BETTER TOGETHER

FINISHED QUILT: 60″ × 78″ • FINISHED BLOCK: 9″ × 9″

Better Together, 60″ × 78″, pieced and quilted by Diane D. Knott

Log cabin quilts can be made in so many variations that I always have fun coming back to this traditional block. I know this won't be my last version, but this one might be my favorite!

MATERIALS
for Twin-Size Quilt*

White print: 1¼ yards for triangles

Pink: 1¼ yards for triangles

Light prints: 2¼ yards total**

Bright prints: 2½ yards total**

Backing: 5 yards

Binding: ⅝ yard

Batting: 68″ × 86″

* See the chart Alternative Quilt Sizes (page 48) to make this quilt in crib, full/queen, or king size.

** Instead of working with yardage, you can use assorted fabrics you have and simply cut the required number of strips noted in the cutting list for each fabric.

CUTTING

White print and pink

Note: Layer white print and pink strips right sides together before cutting.

- Cut 17 strips 3½″ × 18″.
  Cut 136 triangle sets (see Making Triangles from Strips, page 26).

Light prints

- Cut 48 total strips 1½″ × 8½″.
- Cut 48 total strips 1½″ × 7½″.
- Cut 48 total strips 1½″ × 6½″.
- Cut 48 total strips 1½″ × 5½″.
- Cut 48 total strips 1½″ × 4½″.
- Cut 48 total strips 1½″ × 3½″.

Dark prints

- Cut 48 total strips 1½″ × 9½″.
- Cut 48 total strips 1½″ × 8½″.
- Cut 48 total strips 1½″ × 7½″.
- Cut 48 total strips 1½″ × 6½″.
- Cut 48 total strips 1½″ × 5½″.
- Cut 48 total strips 1½″ × 4½″.

Binding

- Cut 8 strips 2″ × width of fabric, or use your preferred width for binding.

ALTERNATIVE QUILT SIZES

	CRIB 42″ × 60″	FULL/QUEEN 78″ × 78″	KING 96″ × 96″
White print	1¼ yards	1¼ yards	1¾ yards
Pink	1¼ yards	1¼ yards	1¾ yards
Light prints	1¼ yards total	3 yards total	4¾ yards total
Bright prints	1½ yards total	3½ yards total	5¼ yards total
Blocks (9″ × 9″)	24 blocks, arranged 4 blocks × 6 blocks	64 blocks, arranged 8 blocks × 8 blocks	100 blocks, arranged 10 blocks × 10 blocks
Backing	3 yards (pieced crosswise)	7¼ yards	8¾ yards
Binding	½ yard	¾ yard	¾ yard
Batting	50″ × 68″	86″ × 86″	104″ × 104″

BLOCK ASSEMBLY

Always use a ¼″ seam allowance. Arrows indicate the pressing direction.

1. Sew the white and pink half-square triangles together (see Making Half-Square Triangles from Strips, page 26). Make 136. Set aside 88 units for the borders. *Fig. A*

2. Sew a light 1½″ × 3½″ strip to the half-square triangle. *Fig. B*

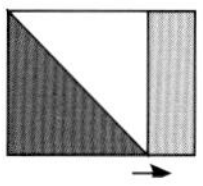

3. Sew a light 1½″ × 4½″ strip to the half-square triangle. *Fig. C*

4. Sew a dark 1½″ × 4½″ strip to the half-square triangle. *Fig. D*

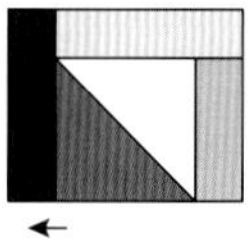

5. Sew a dark 1½″ × 5½″ strip to the half-square triangle. *Fig. E*

6. Sew a light 1½″ × 5½″ strip to the block. *Fig. F*

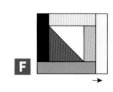

7. Sew a light 1½″ × 6½″ strip to the block. *Fig. G*

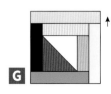

8. Sew a dark 1½″ × 6½″ strip to the block. *Fig. H*

9. Sew a dark 1½″ × 7½″ strip to the block. *Fig. I*

10. Sew a light 1½″ × 7½″ strip to the block. *Fig. J*

11. Sew a light 1½″ × 8½″ strip to the block. *Fig. K*

12. Sew a dark 1½″ × 8½″ strip to the block. *Fig. L*

13. Sew a dark 1½″ × 9½″ strip to the block. Make 48. *Fig. M*

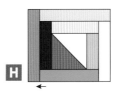
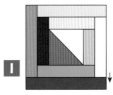
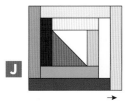
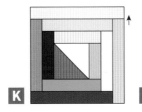
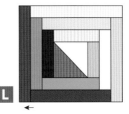
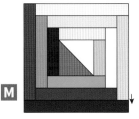

BORDER ASSEMBLY

Sew the half-square triangles into 2 rows of 24 blocks each for the side borders and 2 rows of 20 blocks each for the top and bottom borders. Reverse the direction of the triangles in the center and at the ends. *Fig. N*

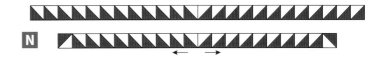

QUILT ASSEMBLY

1. Sew the blocks into 6 vertical rows of 8 blocks each as shown.

2. Sew the rows together.

3. Sew the rows with 24 triangle blocks to the sides of the quilt.

4. Sew the rows with 20 triangle blocks to the top and bottom of the quilt. *Fig. O*

FINISHING

Layer, baste, and quilt as desired. This quilt was quilted with straight lines in the dark strips and free-motion meandering in the light areas. Bind the quilt.

STRIP SECRET
Unify with a Solid

Adding one solid fabric (such as the pink fabric in this quilt) to a wide range of prints can really help organize an otherwise crazy collection.

ECHO

FINISHED QUILT: 80″ × 80″ • FINISHED BLOCK: 10″ × 10″

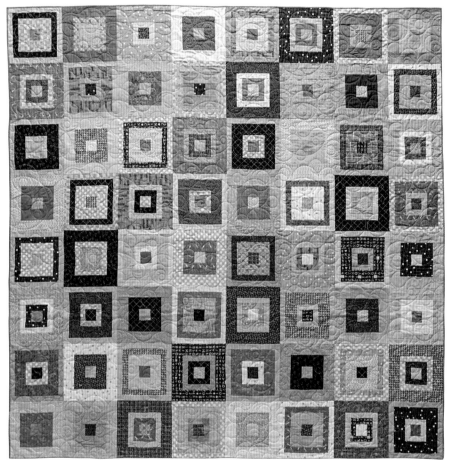

Echo, 80″ × 80″, pieced by Diane D. Knott, quilted by Shawn Lyons Campbell

My son's room needed a summer quilt, and this one was the solution! Minus anything flowery or feminine, this quilt has fresh summery greens, blues, and grays. The blocks actually went together very quickly. I hope my son likes this summer quilt as much as I do.

MATERIALS
for Full/Queen-Size Quilt*

Light prints: 4 yards total**

Bright prints: 3½ yards total**

Backing: 7¾ yards

Binding: ¾ yard

Batting: 88″ × 88″

* See the chart Alternative Quilt Sizes (next page) to make this quilt in crib, twin, or king size.

** Instead of working with yardage, you can use assorted fabrics you have and simply cut the required number of strips noted in the cutting list for each fabric.

CUTTING

Light prints

• Cut 32 total squares 2½″ × 2½″ for block centers.

• From one fabric, cut 16 sets of 2 strips 1½″ × 2½″ and 2 strips 1½″ × 4½″ for Block A.

• From one fabric, cut 16 sets of 2 strips 1½″ × 8½″ and 2 strips 1½″ × 10½″ for Block A.

• From one fabric, cut 16 sets of 2 squares 2½″ × 2½″ and 2 strips 2½″ × 6½″ for Block B.

• From one fabric, cut 16 sets of 2 strips 1½″ × 8½″ and 2 strips 1½″ × 10½″ for Block B.

• From one fabric, cut 16 sets of 2 strips 1½″ × 4½″ and 2 strips 1½″ × 6½″ for Block C.

• From one fabric, cut 16 sets of 2 strips 2½″ × 6½″ and 2 strips 2½″ × 10½″ for Block D.

Bright prints

- Cut 32 total squares 2½″ × 2½″ for block centers.

- From one fabric, cut 16 sets of 2 strips 2½″ × 4½″ and 2 strips 2½″ × 8½″ for Block A.

- From one fabric, cut 16 sets of 2 strips 1½″ × 6½″ and 2 strips 1½″ × 8½″ for Block B.

- From one fabric, cut 16 sets of 2 strips 1½″ × 2½″ and 2 strips 1½″ × 4½″ for Block C.

- From one fabric, cut 16 sets of 2 strips 2½″ × 6½″ and 2 strips 2½″ × 10½″ for Block C.

- From one fabric, cut 16 sets of 2 squares 2½″ × 2½″ and 2 strips 2½″ × 6½″ for Block D.

Binding

- Cut 9 strips 2″ × width of fabric, or use your preferred width for binding.

TIP Cutting Strips

Cut the longest pieces first, so some of the smaller pieces can be cut from the remaining length of the strip.

ALTERNATIVE QUILT SIZES

	CRIB 40″ × 60″	TWIN 60″ × 80″	KING 100″ × 100″
Light prints	1¾ yards total	3¼ yards total	6½ yards total
Bright prints	1½ yards total	2¾ yards total	6 yards total
Blocks (10″ × 10″)	24 blocks, arranged 4 blocks × 6 blocks	48 blocks, arranged 6 blocks × 8 blocks	100 blocks, arranged 10 blocks × 10 blocks
Backing	2¾ yards (pieced crosswise)	5 yards	9 yards
Binding	½ yard	½ yard	¾ yard
Batting	48″ × 68″	68″ × 88″	108″ × 108″

BLOCK ASSEMBLY

Always use a ¼″ seam allowance. Arrows indicate the pressing direction.

Make Block A

1. Sew matching 1½″ × 2½″ light strips to opposite sides of 1 bright center square.

2. Sew matching 1½″ × 4½″ light strips to remaining sides of the bright center square. *Fig. A*

3. Sew matching 2½″ × 4½″ bright strips to opposite sides of the block as shown.

4. Sew matching 2½″ × 8½″ bright strips to opposite sides of the block as shown. *Fig. B*

5. Sew matching 1½″ × 8½″ light strips to opposite sides of the block as shown.

6. Sew matching 1½″ × 10½″ light strips to opposite sides of the block as shown. Make 16. *Fig. C*

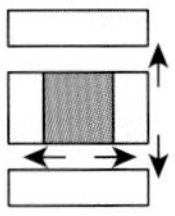

Make Block B

1. Sew matching 2½″ × 2½″ light squares to opposite sides of 1 bright center square.

2. Sew matching 2½″ × 6½″ light strips to remaining sides of the bright center square. *Fig. D*

3. Sew matching 1½″ × 6½″ bright strips to opposite sides of the block as shown.

4. Sew matching 1½″ × 8½″ bright strips to opposite sides of the block as shown. *Fig. E*

5. Sew matching 1½″ × 8½″ light strips to opposite sides of the block as shown.

6. Sew matching 1½″ × 10½″ light strips to opposite sides of the block as shown. Make 16. *Fig. F*

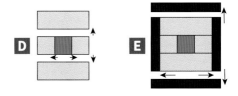
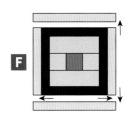

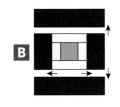
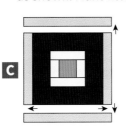

Make Block C

1. Sew matching 1½″ × 2½″ dark strips to opposite sides of 1 light center square.

2. Sew matching 1½″ × 4½″ bright strips to remaining sides of the light center square. *Fig. G*

3. Sew matching 1½″ × 4½″ light strips to opposite sides of the block as shown.

4. Sew matching 1½″ × 6½″ light strips to opposite sides of the block as shown. *Fig. H*

5. Sew matching 2½″ × 6½″ bright strips to opposite sides of the block as shown.

6. Sew matching 2½″ × 10½″ bright strips to opposite sides of the block as shown. Make 16. *Fig. I*

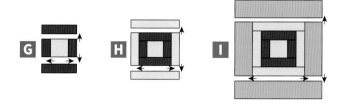

Make Block D

1. Sew matching 2½″ × 2½″ bright squares to opposite sides of 1 light center square.

2. Sew matching 2½″ × 6½″ bright strips to remaining sides of the light center square. *Fig. J*

3. Sew matching 2½″ × 6½″ light strips to opposite sides of the block as shown.

4. Sew matching 2½″ × 10½″ light strips to opposite sides of the block as shown. Make 16. *Fig. K*

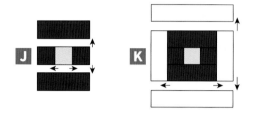

QUILT ASSEMBLY

1. Arrange the blocks as shown, alternating light and bright center squares. (The right half of the quilt continues the block arrangement as shown on the left half.)

2. Sew 8 rows of 8 blocks each.

3. Sew the rows into pairs, then sew the pairs together. *Fig. L*

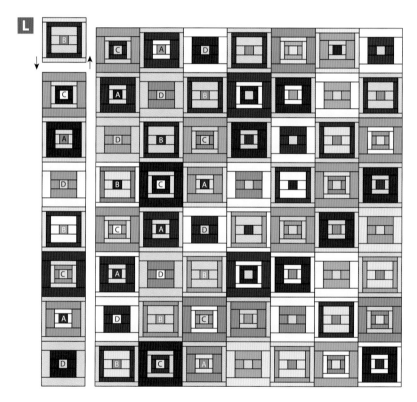

FINISHING

Layer, baste, and quilt as desired. Bind the quilt.

STRIP SECRET
Precut Strips Option

To use only precut 2½″ strips, make the quilt using only 32 Block D and 32 Block D reversing the color placement.

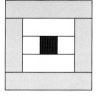

TOWNHOUSE ROW

FINISHED QUILT: 66″ × 66″ • FINISHED BLOCK: 6″ × 6″

Townhouse Row, 66″ × 66″, pieced by Diane D. Knott, quilted by Cheryl Ashley-Serafine

This quilt is made from two fat quarter bundles and a single red fabric. These homespun fabrics are favorites of mine. Choose a bundle or two of your favorites for your own unique style!

MATERIALS
for Crib-Size Quilt*

Red: ¾ yard

Light prints: 2¼ yards total**

Dark prints: 4 yards total**

Backing: 4¼ yards

Binding: ½ yard

Batting: 74″ × 74″

* See the chart Alternative Quilt Sizes (page 54) to make this quilt in twin, full/queen, or king size.

** Instead of working with yardage, you can use assorted fabrics you have and simply cut the required number of strips noted in the cutting list for each fabric.

CUTTING

Red

• Cut 121 squares 2½″ × 2½″ for Log Cabin block centers and house windows.

Light prints

• Cut 81 total strips 1½″ × 10″. Subcut into 1½″ × 4½″ and 1½″ × 5½″ strips.

• Cut 81 total strips 1½″ × 6″. Subcut into 1½″ × 2½″ and 1½″ × 3½″ strips.

• Cut 36 total strips 2½″ × 5″. Subcut into 2 squares 2½″ × 2½″ for the sky of house blocks.

• Cut 36 total strips 1½″ × 3½″ for door of house blocks.

Dark prints

• Cut 85 total strips 1½″ × 12″. Subcut into 1½″ × 5½″ and 1½″ × 6½″ strips.

• Cut 85 total strips 1½″ × 8″. Subcut into 1½″ × 3½″ and 1½″ × 4½″ strips.

• Cut 4 total strips 1½″ × 10″. Subcut into 1½″ × 4½″ and 1½″ × 5½″ strips for corner blocks.

• Cut 4 total strips 1½″ × 6″. Subcut into 1½″ × 2½″ and 1½″ × 3½″ strips for corner blocks.

• Cut 72 total strips 1½″ × 6½″ for roof of house blocks.

• Cut 1 strip 1½″ × 6½″, 1 strip 1½″ × 2½″, and 3 strips 1½″ × 3½″ for each of 36 house blocks.

Binding

• Cut 7 strips 2″ × width of fabric, or use your preferred width for binding.

ALTERNATIVE QUILT SIZES

	TWIN 66″ × 78″	FULL/QUEEN 84″ × 84″	KING 102″ × 102″
Red	⅞ yard	1¼ yards	1½ yards
Light prints	2½ yards total	3½ yards total	4¾ yards total
Dark prints	3 yards total	4¼ yards total	6 yards total
Blocks (6″ × 6″): Log Cabin, house, and corner	99 Log Cabin blocks, 40 house blocks, and 4 corner blocks, arranged 11 blocks × 13 blocks	144 Log Cabin blocks, 48 house blocks, and 4 corner blocks, arranged 14 blocks × 14 blocks	225 Log Cabin blocks, 60 house blocks, and 4 corner blocks, arranged 17 blocks × 17 blocks
Backing	5 yards	7¾ yards	9¼ yards
Binding	½ yard	¾ yard	¾ yard
Batting	74″ × 86″	92″ × 92″	110″ × 110″

BLOCK ASSEMBLY

Always use a ¼″ seam allowance. • *Arrows indicate the pressing direction.*

Make Main Log Cabin Blocks

1. Sew a 1½″ × 2½″ light strip to a red square. *Fig. A*

2. Sew the same fabric 1½″ × 3½″ light strip to the red square unit as shown. *Fig. B*

3. Sew a 1½″ × 3½″ dark strip to the red square unit as shown. *Fig. C*

4. Sew the same fabric 1½″ × 4½″ dark strip to the red square unit as shown. *Fig. D*

5. Sew a 1½″ × 4½″ light strip to the block. *Fig. E*

6. Sew the same fabric 1½″ × 5½″ light strip to the block. *Fig. F*

7. Sew a 1½″ × 5½″ dark strip to the block. *Fig. G*

8. Sew the same fabric 1½″ × 6½″ dark strip to the block. Make 81. *Fig. H*

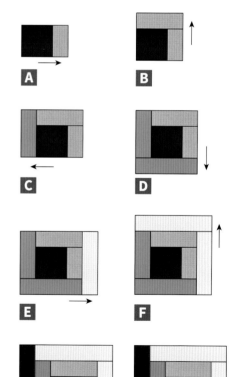

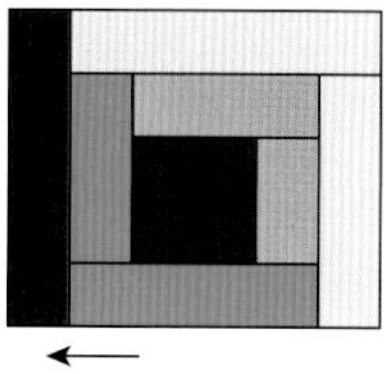

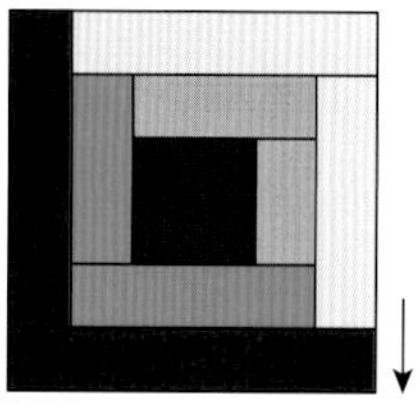

Make Border Corner Log Cabin Blocks

Follow the instructions for the main Log Cabin block substituting dark strips in place of the light strips. Make 4 blocks. *Fig. I*

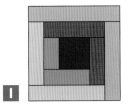

Make House Block Borders

1. Sew 2 roof strips 1½″ × 6½″ together. *Fig. J*

2. Mark the back of matching light (sky) squares on the diagonal. Place these at the ends of the roof strips and sew along the marked line. Cut away the excess. *Figs. K & L*

3. Sew a 1½″ × 2½″ house strip to a red square.

4. Sew a 1½″ × 3½″ house strip to the red square unit. *Fig. M*

5. Sew 1½″ × 3½″ house strips to both sides of the 1½″ × 3½″ door strip.

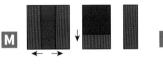

6. Sew these 2 units together. *Fig. N*

7. Sew a 1½″ × 6½″ house strip to the top edge of the house unit.

8. Sew the roof unit to the house unit. Make 36 blocks. *Fig. O*

QUILT ASSEMBLY

1. Sew the Log Cabin blocks into 9 rows of 9 blocks each as shown.

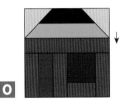

2. Sew the rows together in groups of three. Join the rows.

3. Sew the house blocks into 4 borders of 9 blocks each.

4. Sew 2 house block borders to the sides of the quilt.

5. Sew the corner Log Cabin blocks to the ends of the remaining house block borders.

6. Sew the house block rows borders to the top and bottom of the quilt. *Fig. P*

FINISHING

Layer, baste, and quilt as desired. This quilt features an allover pattern. Bind the quilt.

 **Mix It Up**

Change this quilt by substituting any 6″ block, or a variety of blocks, to replace the house blocks to create your own personalized quilt.

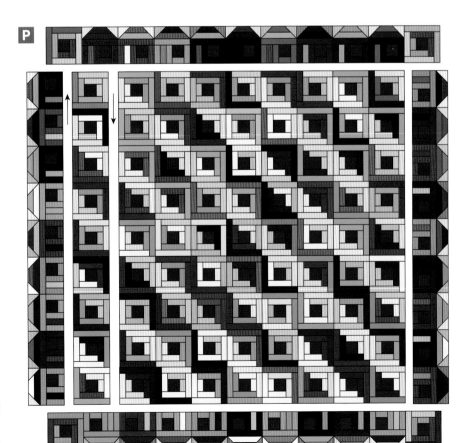

Piecing Alternatives

Sometimes strips become scraps. Either they've been miscut, the edge of the fabric is uneven, or—let's face it— accidents happen! So what's a quilter to do with strips that are missing a sliver or that may not be long enough for another project? What should you do with all the pieces of leftover strips that are too short for much of anything? Here are a few piecing alternatives to put those strip scraps to use.

SEWING STRIPS ON A FOUNDATION

If you have strips that were miscut or are slightly off for any reason, sewing them to a foundation is the answer! This method will secure them in place, and the end result will be a block that is always the perfect size no matter the variations of strips used. As long as you are covering the foundation completely, the block will be the right size even if your strips are not. *Diamonds Are Forever* (page 58) uses this method.

When using a foundation for sewing strips, always start with a thin layer of fabric or muslin cut to the desired size.

1. Cut and mark the foundation. The foundation can be marked with washable or permanent markers since the marks will be covered with fabric.

2. Layer the first two strips and sew right sides together.

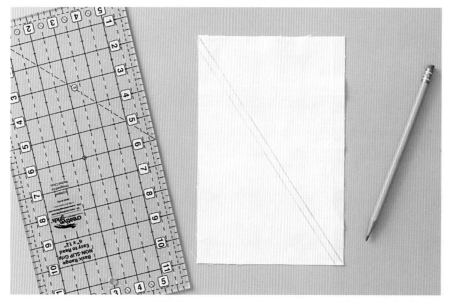

3. Flip the strips open and press. Take care when pressing the seams to ensure they are completely opened and flat.

4. Layer another strip along the edge and repeat. Continue until the foundation is covered. Trim the edges once all of the strips are added.

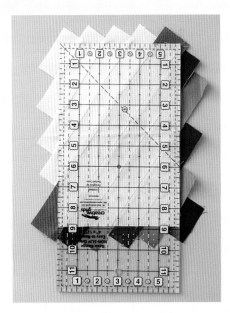

STRIP SECRET
Foundation Options

The foundation for your strips can be either paper or fabric. When using a paper foundation for sewing, the paper must be removed after the fabrics are sewn together. When using a fabric foundation, the layer of fabric remains in the quilt, adding another layer to the quilt. Using fabric offers the option of using a thinner batting, a single flannel layer, or no batting at all. *Diamonds Are Forever* (page 58) has fabric foundations and no batting to make hand quilting quick and easy.

SEWING SCRAPS INTO STRIPS

There are going to be leftover bits of strips no matter which quilt you choose to make. It's just the nature of quilting that there will be scraps left. But why waste those leftover strips ends and scraps? Sewing them together to make larger strips is fun and easy. It's a perfect project for a rainy day when you have no other plans. Just sew and sew and sew, and before you know it, you'll have strips, and then your strips will become blocks. Just keep adding to it from time to time, and you'll be surprised how quickly your tiniest scraps become a colorful quilt!

1. Chain sew the scraps together in pairs. Press the seams.

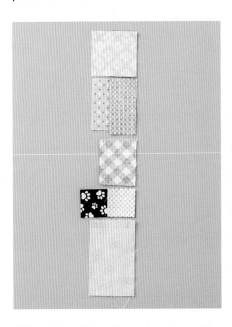

2. Sew the pairs together.

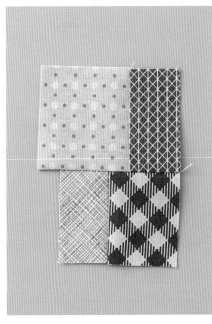

3. Continue sewing pairs to the ends of the unit until piece is at least the desired size, then trim the edges.

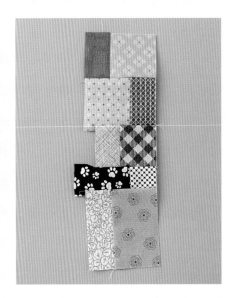

DIAMONDS ARE FOREVER

FINISHED QUILT: 48″ × 72″ • FINISHED BLOCK: 8″ × 12″

Diamonds Are Forever, 48″ × 72″, pieced and hand quilted by Diane D. Knott

Having some imperfect strips left over from other projects, I knew this quilt would be the perfect home for them. The foundation ensures that even wonky strips will be tamed. Sometimes, a strip is too narrow or has a wayward edge, but don't toss the whole strip—save it for this method! Hand quilting is so relaxing, and this quilt spent lots of time in my lap while I stitched it. Perhaps it should be named **Diamonds Take Forever***?*

MATERIALS
for Crib-Size Quilt*

Muslin: 3 yards

Pink: 1 yard

Dark prints: 2¾ yards total**

Light prints: 2¼ yards total**

Backing: 3¼ yards
(pieced crosswise)

Binding: ½ yard

Batting: 56″ × 80″

* See the chart Alternative Quilt Sizes (next page) to make this quilt in twin, full/queen, or king size.

** Instead of working with yardage, you can use assorted fabrics you have and simply cut the required number of strips noted in the cutting list for each fabric.

CUTTING

Muslin

• Cut 36 rectangles 8½″ × 12½″.

Pink

• Cut 36 strips 1½″ × 15″.

Dark prints

• Cut 36 total strips 2″ × 15″.

• Cut 36 total strips 2″ × 12″.

• Cut 36 total strips 2″ × 9″.

• Cut 36 total strips 2″ × 6″.

• Cut 36 total strips 2″ × 3″.

Light prints

• Cut 36 total strips 2″ × 13″.

• Cut 36 total strips 2″ × 10″.

• Cut 36 total strips 2″ × 7″.

• Cut 36 total strips 2″ × 4″.

Binding

• Cut 7 strips 2″ × width of fabric, or use your preferred width for binding.

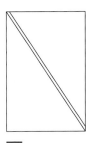

A

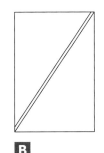

B

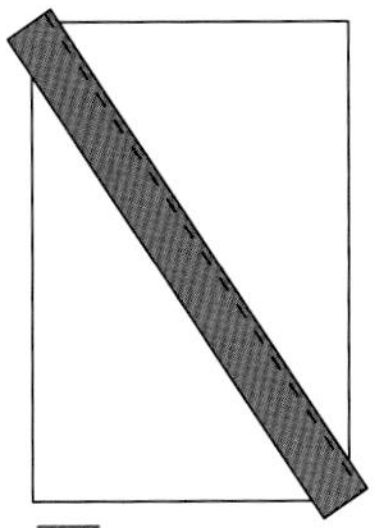

C

ALTERNATIVE QUILT SIZES

	TWIN 64″ × 84″	FULL/QUEEN 80″ × 84″	KING 96″ × 108″
Muslin	4½ yards	6 yards	9 yards
Pink	1½ yards	1½ yards	2½ yards
Dark prints	3¾ yards total	5 yards total	7½ yards total
Light prints	3½ yards total	4½ yards total	6½ yards total
Blocks (8″ × 12″)	28 blocks and 28 reverse blocks arranged, 8 blocks × 7 blocks	35 blocks and 35 reverse blocks, arranged 10 blocks × 7 blocks	54 blocks and 54 reverse blocks, arranged 12 blocks × 9 blocks
Backing	5¼ yards	7½ yards (pieced crosswise)	8¾ yards (pieced crosswise)
Binding	½ yard	¾ yard	¾ yard
Batting	72″ × 92″	88″ × 92″	104″ × 116″

BLOCK ASSEMBLY

Always use a ¼″ seam allowance. • *Arrows indicate the pressing direction.*

Mark Foundation

1. Mark a diagonal line on the foundation from the upper left corner to lower right corner as shown.

2. Mark a second line ¼″ to the right of the first line as shown. Make 18 blocks. *Fig. A*

3. To make reverse blocks, mark a diagonal line on the foundation from the upper right corner to the lower left corner as shown.

4. Mark a second line ¼″ to the left of the first line as shown. Make 18 reverse blocks. *Fig. B*

Sew Strips on Foundation

1. Layer a pink strip and a dark 2″ × 15″ strip right sides together.

2. Place the layered strips on the block, with the pink strip next to the foundation.

3. Line up the right edge of the strip set with the second line marked.

4. Sew the strips to the foundation. With the edges of the strips on the second diagonal line, the seam will be exactly on the first line. *Fig. C*

5. Open the top strip and press. Center a dark 2˝ × 12˝ strip on top of the previous dark strip and sew. *Fig. D*

6. Open and press. Continue sewing and pressing, using a strip the next size shorter each time. *Figs. E & F*

7. Rotate the block and sew the light strips in the same manner, starting with the longest strip. *Figs. G & H*

8. Turn the block over and trim the strips to the edge of the foundation. Make 18 blocks and 18 reverse blocks. *Fig. I*

QUILT ASSEMBLY

1. Arrange the blocks and reverse blocks as shown.

2. Sew the blocks together into sets of 4 to create diamond units.

3. Sew the diamond units into 3 rows of 3 diamond units.

4. Sew the rows together. *Fig. J*

FINISHING

Layer, baste, and quilt as desired. This quilt was hand quilted with pearl cotton thread in the big stitch style. There is no batting in this quilt, just the patchwork, foundation layer, and backing. Bind the quilt.

STRIP SECRET
Quilting with Foundation

When making a quilt using a fabric foundation, consider skipping the batting, or substitute a thin flannel for easier hand quilting.

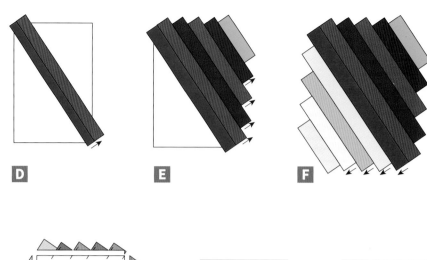

D   E   F

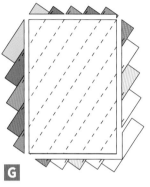

G   H   I

J

WASH DAY

FINISHED QUILT: 52½″ × 77½″ • FINISHED BLOCK: 10″ × 10″

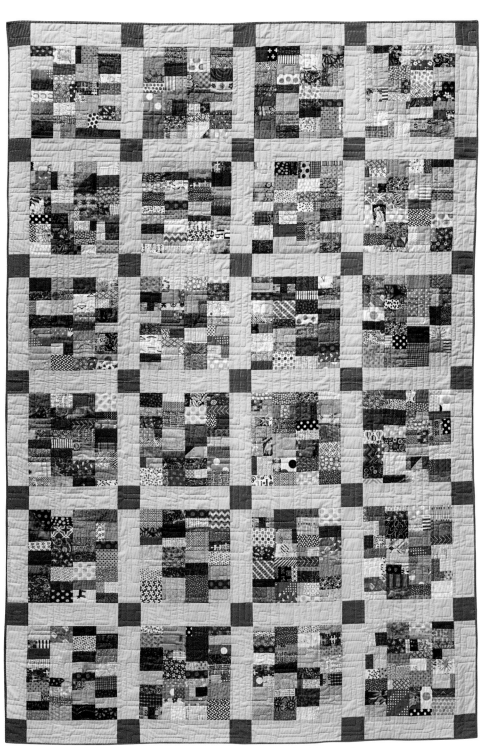

After making a few strip quilts, the tiny pieces of leftover strips begin to pile up. What can be done with all the little trimmings and leftover pieces? Sew them into bigger strips of course! This quilt is a bit of memory quilt, as it has tiny bits of many other quilts in it. It's the perfect solution for those of us who can't stand to throw any fabric away! To me, each block looked like a basket of laundry waiting to be folded, hence the name.

MATERIALS
for Twin-Size Quilt*

Green: 1¾ yards

Pink: ⅜ yard

Scraps: 3 yards total

Backing: 5 yards

Binding: ½ yard

Batting: 60″ × 85″

* See the chart Alternative Quilt Sizes (page 62) to make this quilt in crib, full/queen, or king size.

Wash Day, 52½″ × 77½″, pieced by Diane D. Knott, quilted by Cheryl Ashley-Serafine

CUTTING

Green

• Cut 58 strips 3″ × 10½″
  for sashing.

Pink

• Cut 35 squares 3″ × 3″
  for cornerstones.

Binding

• Cut 7 strips 2″ × width of fabric, or
  use your preferred width for binding.

ALTERNATIVE QUILT SIZES

	CRIB 52½″ × 52½″	FULL/QUEEN 90″ × 90″	KING 102½″ × 90″
Green	1½ yards	3 yards	3½ yards
Pink	⅓ yard	⅝ yard	¾ yards
Scraps	2 yards total	6 yards total	7 yards total
Blocks (10″ × 10″)	16 blocks, arranged 4 blocks × 4 blocks	49 blocks, arranged 7 blocks × 7 blocks	56 blocks, arranged 8 blocks × 7 blocks
Backing	3½ yards	8¼ yards	8¼ yards (pieced crosswise)
Binding	½ yard	¾ yard	¾ yard
Batting	60″ × 60″	98″ × 98″	108″ × 98″

BLOCK ASSEMBLY

Always use a ¼″ seam allowance. • Arrows indicate the pressing direction.

1. Chain sew the smallest scraps together (see Sewing Scraps into Strips, page 57). *Fig. A*

2. Sew the pieced units to larger scraps and to each other to create strips at least 3″ × 10½″. *Fig. B*

3. Trim the sewn scraps into strips 3″ × 10½″. Make 96 pieced strips. *Fig. C*

4. Sew 4 strips together lengthwise to make a 10½″ × 10½″ block. Make 24. *Fig. D*

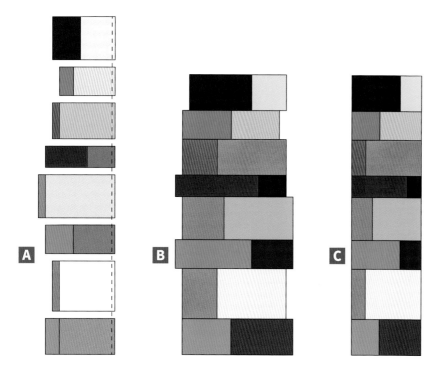

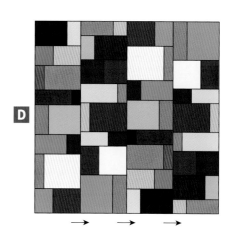

A B C D

QUILT ASSEMBLY

1. Sew 7 cornerstone squares and 6 vertical sashing strips together as shown. Make 5.

2. Sew 7 horizontal sashing strips and 6 blocks together as shown. Make 4.

3. Sew the sashing rows and block rows together as shown. *Fig. E*

FINISHING

Layer, baste, and quilt as desired. This quilt features a pattern that mimics the shapes in the blocks. Bind the quilt.

STRIP SECRET
Use Those Scraps

Sew the smallest of scraps together and keep them in a basket. Add to the basket over time and once the basket is full, start sewing the units into strips. This makes a great ongoing project that uses up scraps as they are created and keeps the sewing room tidy as well!

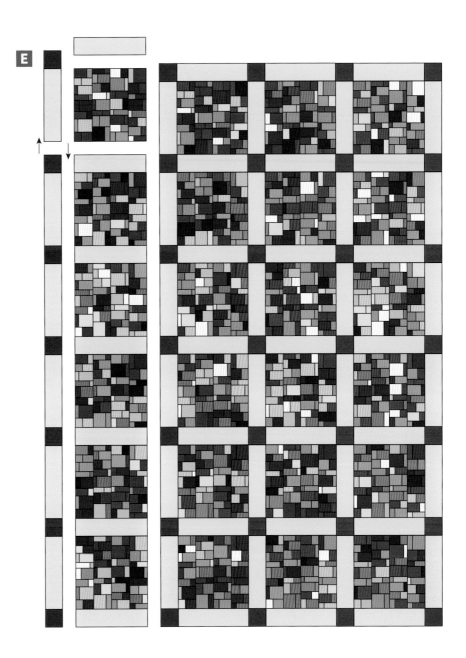

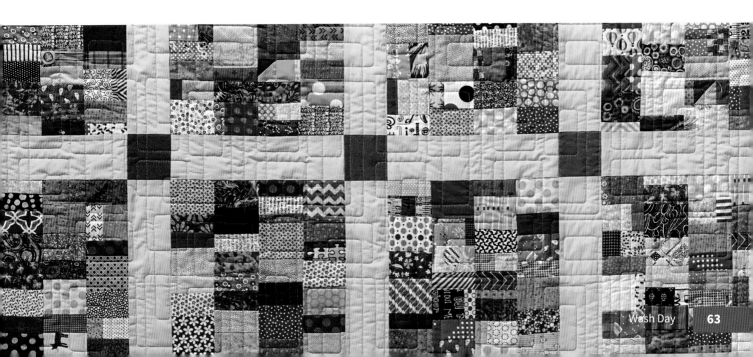

Selvages

In recent years, fabric companies have taken note of how much quilters love to use selvages. What once was a throw-away portion of the fabric has become another fun feature for quilters who are seeking creative ways to use these fabric edges. Long gone are the days of simple printed words and color dots on selvages. Today a quilter can expect to find adorable motifs in place of color dots and stylized labels and fonts for the written information. With all the creative design going into selvages, it only makes sense to feature them in a project.

SEWING SELVAGES

Sewing selvages do not require a ¼″ seam allowance. The finished edge of the selvage (from the edge of the bolt) is layered on top of the cut edge of the next selvage. Top stitching along the finished edge will secure the two selvages together. Sew as close as you can to the woven edge, leaving a ¼″ seam allowance on the raw edge of the selvage strip underneath.

1. Layer the woven edge of one selvage over the raw edge of another selvage. Sew together along the woven edge of the top selvage.

2. Repeat until the sewn unit is desired size then trim the edges.

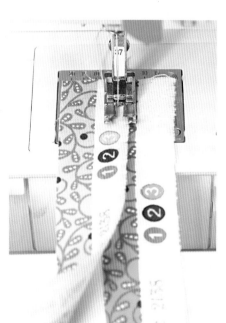

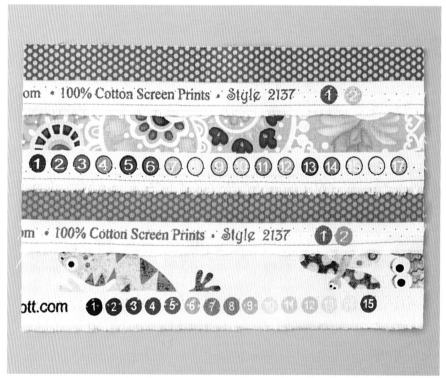

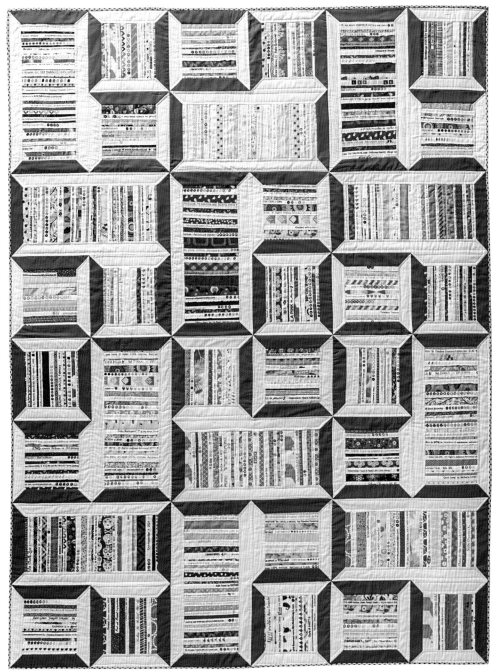

SELVAGE SPOOLS

FINISHED QUILT: 54″ × 72″ • FINISHED BLOCKS: 9″ × 9″ and 9″ × 18″

Selvage Spools, 54″ × 72″, pieced and quilted by Diane D. Knott

I've made quite a few selvage quilts and this might be my favorite. Sorting the selvages into colorways was so fun! I know I have more selvage quilts in my future.

MATERIALS

for Twin-Size Quilt*

Gray: 1¼ yards

White print: 1¾ yards

Selvages: 348 pieces 6½″ × 1″
(or fewer pieces if cut wider)

Backing: 3½ yards
(pieced crosswise)

Binding: ½ yard

Batting: 62″ × 80″

* See the chart Alternative Quilt
Sizes (page 66) to make this quilt
in crib, full/queen, or king size.

CUTTING

Gray

• Cut 72 strips 2″ × 9½″.

White print

• Cut 48 strips 2″ × 9½″ for background.

• Cut 24 strips 2″ × 18½″ for background.

Binding

• Cut 7 strips 2″ × width of fabric, or your preferred width for binding.

ALTERNATIVE QUILT SIZES

	CRIB 54″ × 54″	FULL/QUEEN 90″ × 90″	KING 108″ × 90″
Gray	1 yard	1¼ yards	1½ yards
White print	1¼ yards	3 yards	3¼ yards
Selvages	261 pieces 6½″ × 1″ (or fewer pieces if cut wider)	696 pieces 6½″ × 1″ (or fewer pieces if cut wider)	870 pieces 6½″ × 1″ (or fewer pieces if cut wider)
Blocks (9″ × 9″ and 9″ × 18″)	18 small and 9 large blocks, arranged 3 units × 3 units	50 small and 25 large blocks, arranged 5 units × 5 units	60 small and 30 large blocks, arranged 6 units × 5 units
Backing	3¾ yards	8¼ yards	8¼ yards (pieced crosswise)
Binding	½ yard	¾ yard	¾ yard
Batting	62″ × 62″	98″ × 98″	116″ × 98″

BLOCK ASSEMBLY

Always use a ¼″ seam allowance. • *Arrows indicate the pressing direction.*

Make Strip Sets

1. Sew the selvages together (see Sewing Selvages, page 64).

2. Trim the joined selvages to 6½″ × 6½″ for the small blocks. Make 24.

3. Trim the joined selvages to 6½″ × 15½″ for the large blocks. Make 12.

Make Small Blocks

1. To make the blocks, you will need to sew mitered corners. Arrange a 6½″ × 6½″ selvage unit and the 2″ × 9½″ background strips so that the strips extend 1½″ beyond the ends of the selvage unit.

2. Sew, beginning and ending ¼″ from the corner of the selvage unit. Backstitch to secure the seams. *Fig. A*

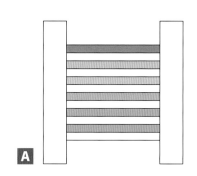

A

3. Fold the background strips out of the way and sew the 2″ × 9½″ gray strips in the same manner as in Step 1. *Fig. B*

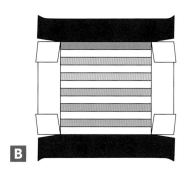

B

4. Fold the block in half on the diagonal with right sides together and with the ends of the background strips lined up. Mark a sewing line on the background strip from the corner of the strip end to the intersection of the seams on the selvage unit. *Fig. C*

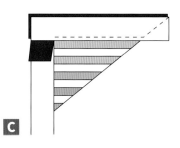

C

5. Sew on the drawn line from the corner to the inter-section, backstitching to secure the seams. Repeat on all 4 corners. Trim the excess fabric ¼″ beyond the seam. Make 24.

6. Press from the back and pinwheel the seams at the intersections. Turn over and press from the front. *Fig. D*

Make Large Blocks

Sew the large blocks in the same manner as the small ones, using a 6½″ × 15½″ selvage unit with 2 background 2″ × 18½″ strips and 2 gray 2″ × 9½″ strips. Make 12. *Fig. E*

QUILT ASSEMBLY

1. Arrange the blocks as shown. Note that the blocks are rotated so that the gray strips are not next to one another.

2. Sew 2 small blocks together, and then sew a large block to one side of the 2 small blocks. Make 12 units.

3. Sew the units into rows. Sew the rows together. *Fig. F*

FINISHING

Layer, baste, and quilt as desired. This quilt was machine quilted in straight lines along the selvage pieces and between blocks. Bind the quilt.

STRIP SECRET
Let Your Colors Show

Using a variety of widths when cutting selvages will allow more color to show and create more interesting results.

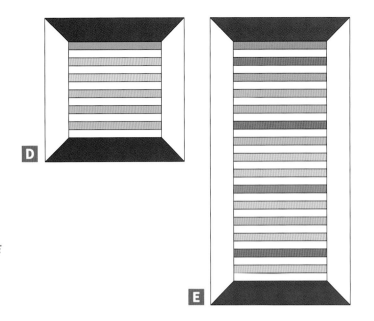

BLANKS
for Coloring

Have a little fun choosing color options with these coloring pages. Print and color your next quilt to preview what your fabric choices will look like before taking the first stitch. Or just print and color for fun!

SHIMMER (quilt photo, page 17)

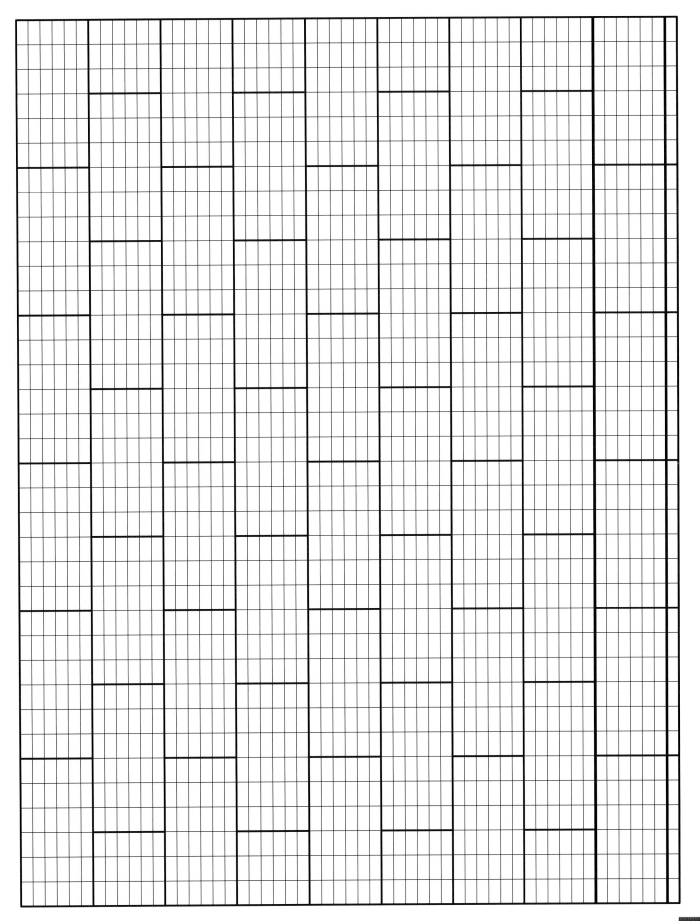

CHAIN REACTION (quilt photo, page 20)

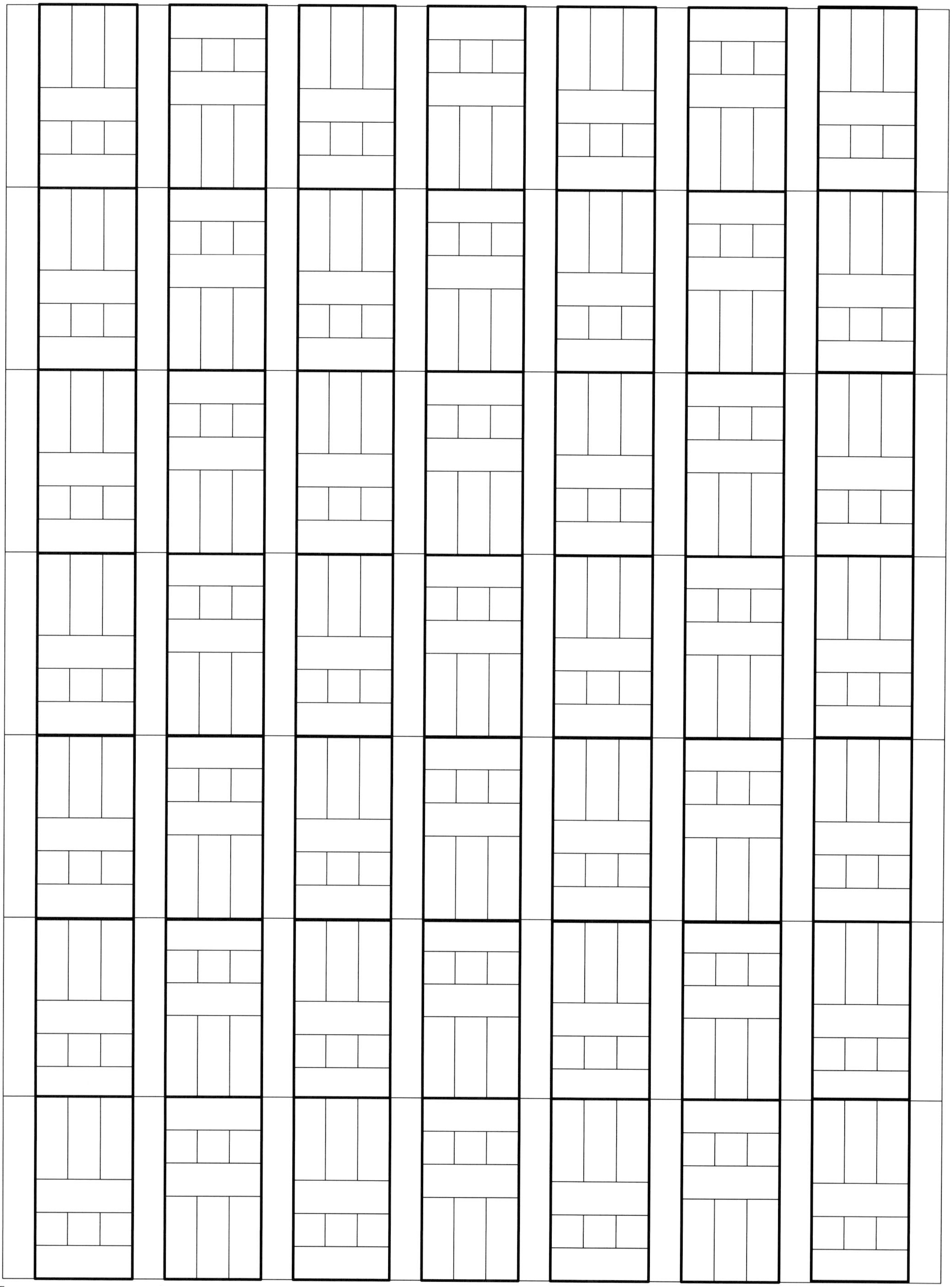

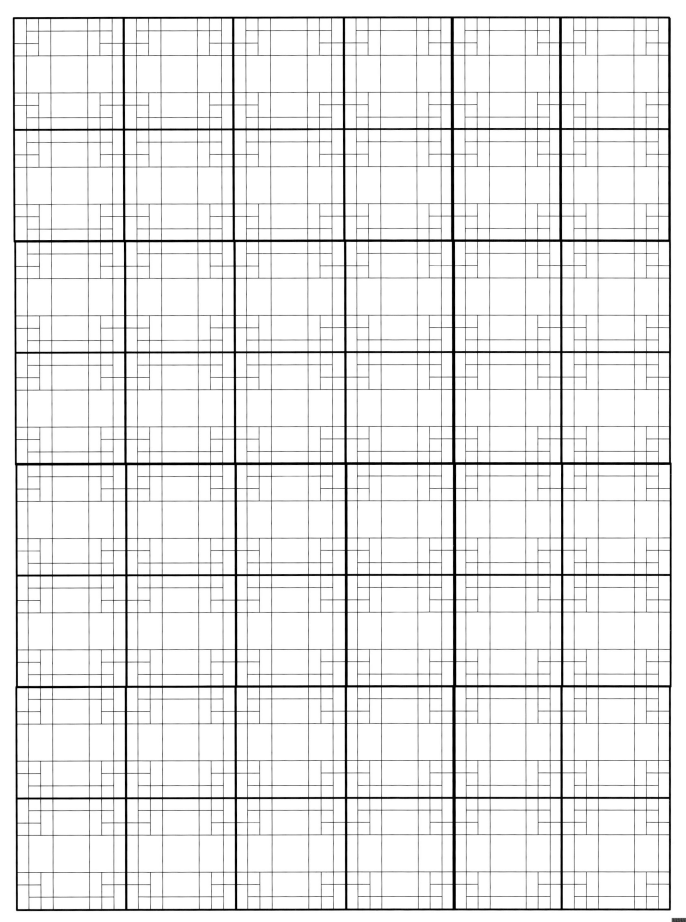

SPLASH (quilt photo, page 27)

AUNT ELSIE (quilt photo, page 30)

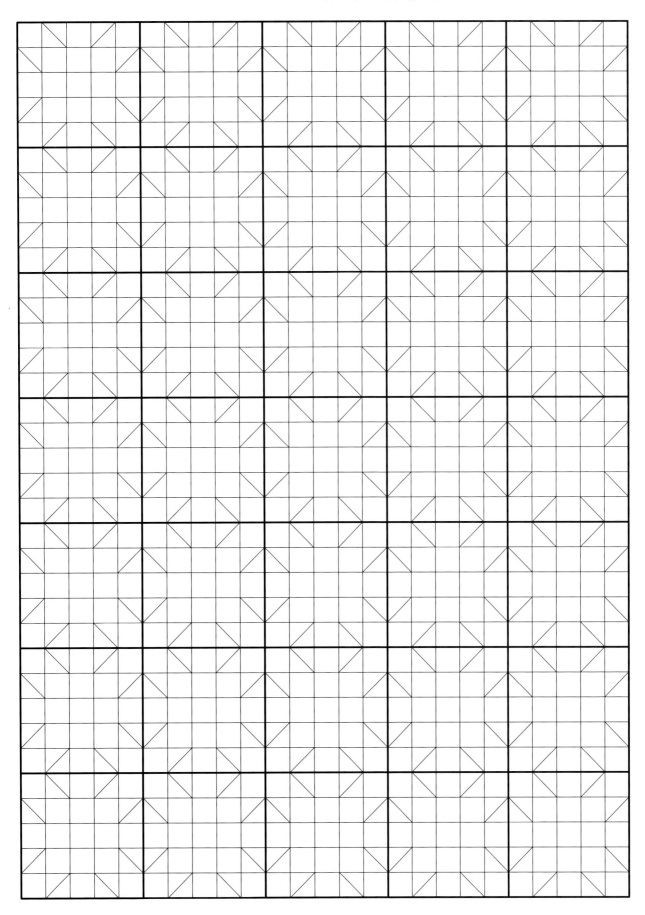

FIESTA (quilt photo, page 33)

Strip Quilt Secrets

ONE-WAY TICKET (quilt photo, page 37)

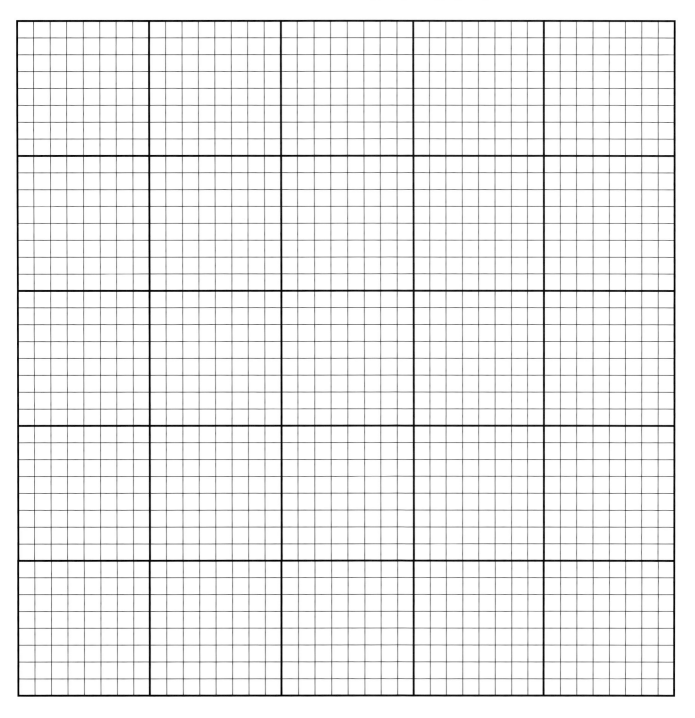

VORTEX (quilt photo, page 43)

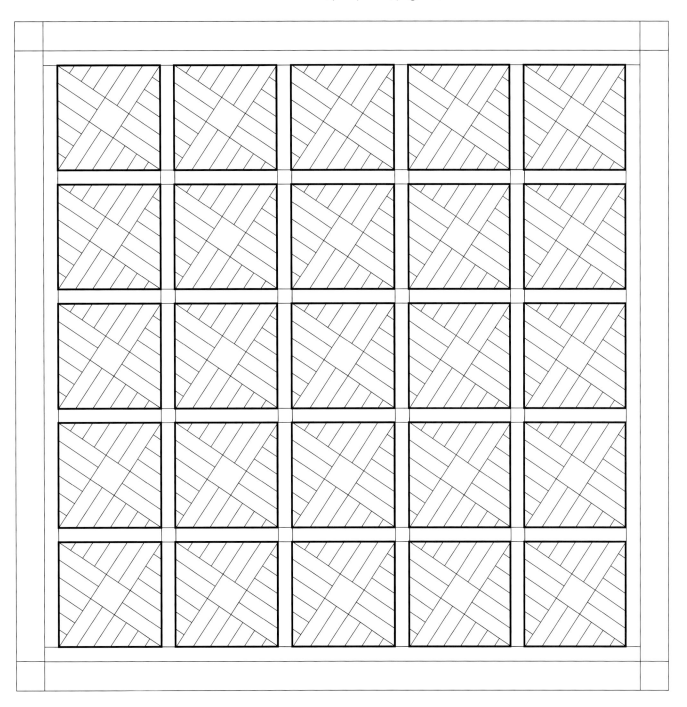

ECHO (quilt photo, page 50)

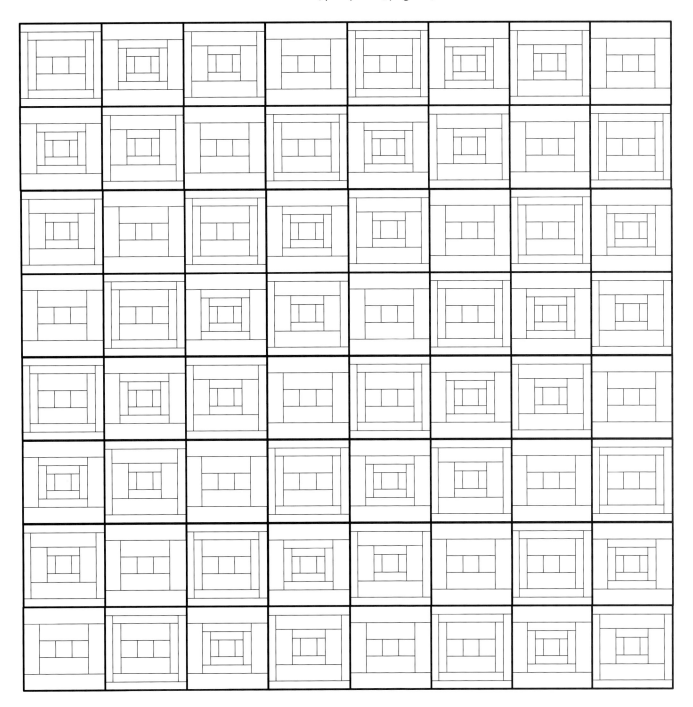

TOWNHOUSE ROW (quilt photo, page 53)

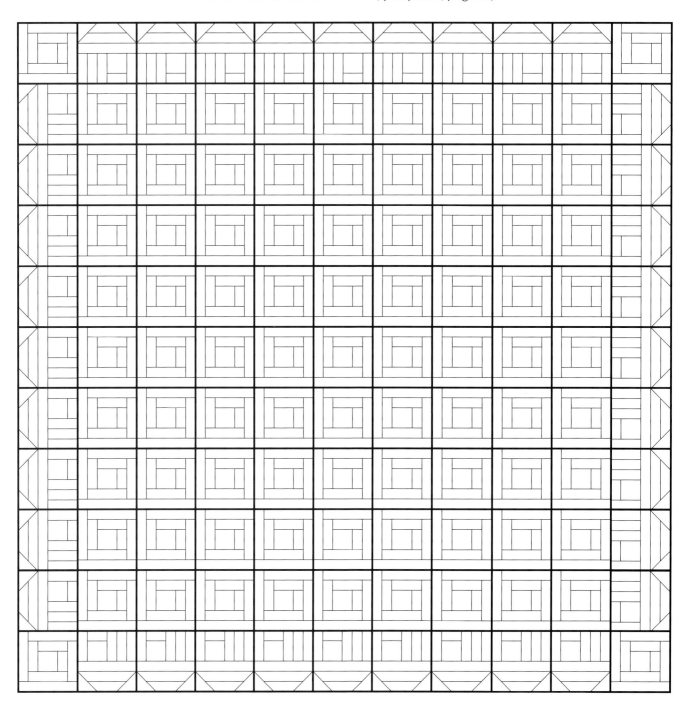

WASH DAY (quilt photo, page 61)

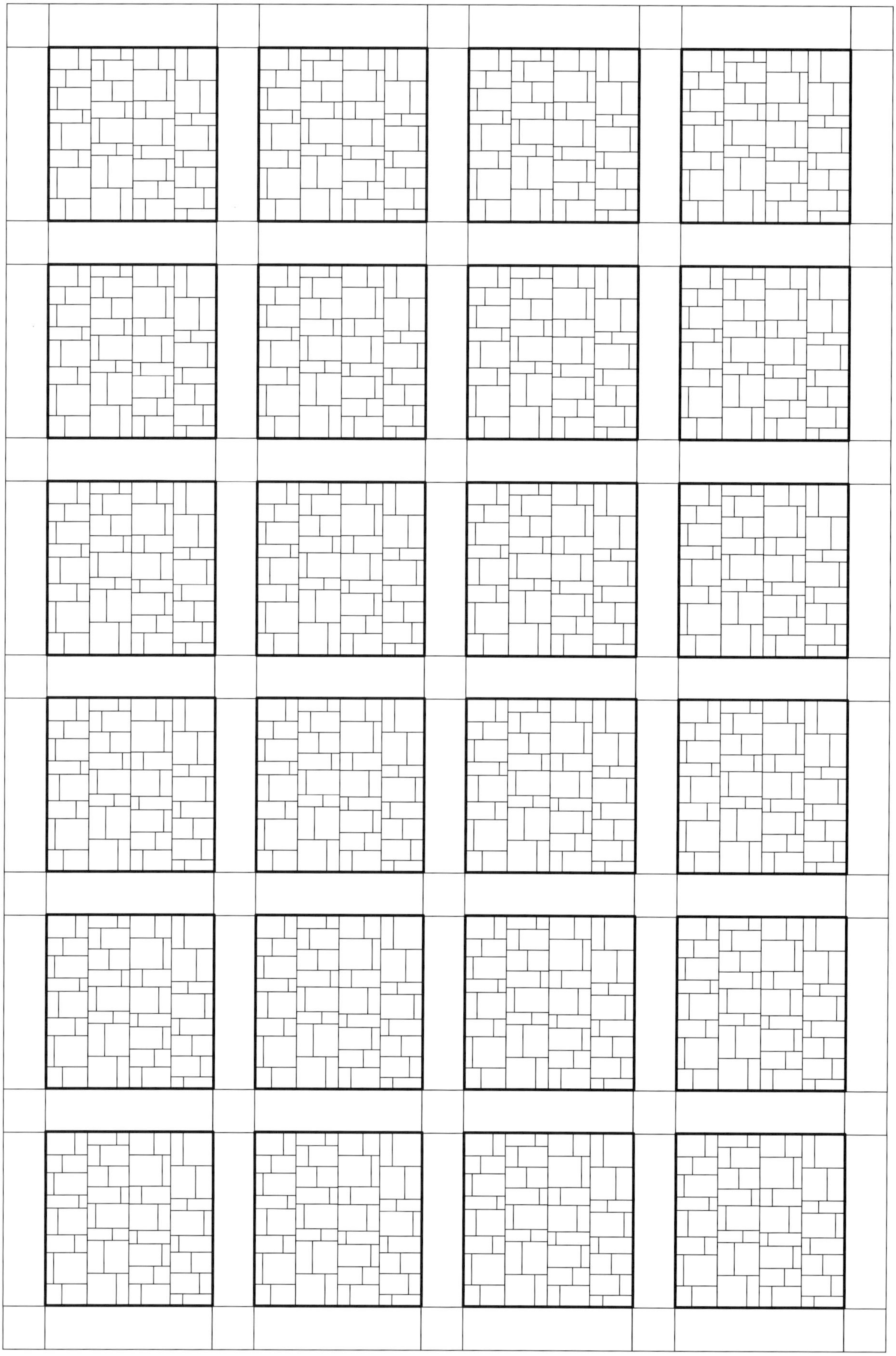

INDEX of Quilts by Strip Size

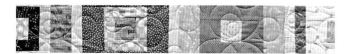

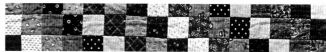
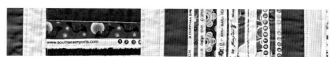

2½″ Strips

Aunt Elsie (page 30)

Chain Reaction (page 20)

Echo (page 50)

Fiesta (page 33)

Lime Twist (page 40)

Shimmer (page 17)

Splash (page 27)

Square Pegs (page 22)

3½″ Strips

Fiesta (page 33)

Square Pegs (page 22)

Vortex (page 43)

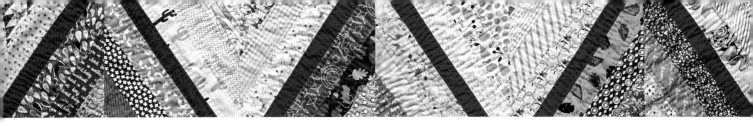

ABOUT THE AUTHOR

Diane D. Knott

When she isn't teaching quilt workshops and working part-time at a local quilt shop, Diane enjoys longarm quilting for others as well as herself. Diane especially enjoys the challenge of creating custom commission quilts for clients. When she's not quilting, Diane likes traveling with her husband, Bill. They have three children, currently attending three different universities, and three very spoiled dogs. Diane is also the author of *Scrap Quilt Secrets* (from C&T Publishing).

Visit Diane online for her teaching schedule and latest news and updates!
Website: butterflythreadsquilting.com

Photo by Kelly M. Knott

Also by Diane D. Knott:

Want even more creative content?

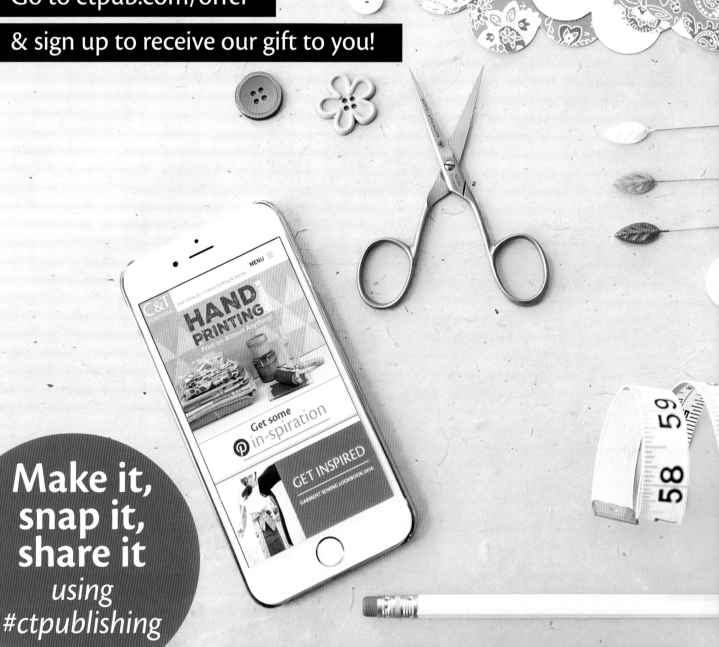

Make it, snap it, share it *using #ctpublishing*